Campagnes de santé publique :
faire passer le message

Public health campaigns:

getting the message across

حملات الصحة العمومية:
تبليغ الرسالة

公共卫生活动:
增进了解

Кампании общественного здравоохранения
доведение информации до тех, кому она предн

D1295758

Campañas de salud pública:
la transmisión del mensaje

World Health Organization

WHO Library Cataloguing-in-Publication Data:

Public health campaigns: getting the message across.

1.Health promotion. 2.Posters. 3.World Health Organization - history. 4.Audiovisual aids. 5.Advertising as topic. I.World Health Organization.

ISBN 978 92 4 056027 7 (soft cover)   (NLM classification: WA 590)
ISBN 978 92 4 056028 4 (hard cover)

© World Health Organization 2009

Printed in Switzerland

Contents

Sommaire

Índice

Содержание

目录

المحتويات

Foreword

Defining what makes an effective poster is not a simple matter. Like any piece of propaganda, it is designed to persuade the viewer to do something – either to buy the product advertised or in the case of the public health poster, to modify or eliminate destructive habits. A poster can implore us to stop smoking, get vaccinated, use condoms or not share needles. At the very least it must make us stop, if only for a few seconds, to absorb its message – a message that typically takes the form of a forceful image accompanied by hard-hitting words.

Despite the widespread use of official public health messages by local and state governments, public health posters were scarce prior to the First World War. However, beginning in 1917, with battles raging across Europe, governments felt that it was necessary to boost the public's health and strength. For example, the French government reacted to concerns about alcoholism, tuberculosis and sexually transmitted diseases among servicemen by creating sustained public campaigns to warn about these dangers. Posters were an integral part of this effort. Their striking appearance and frequently strident language introduced a tone of forceful propaganda. Tuberculosis posters advocated early treatment, warned against sleeping in rooms without open windows, and called for more research funds.

Prominent European artists who created designs for public health campaigns are well known and some are featured in this book. For instance the French artists Lucien Lévy-Dhurmer and Jules-Abel Faivre set high standards during the First World War and their work is timeless as a result. Other well-known poster artists include Ramón Casas, Franz von Stuck, Adolph Hohenstein, Louis Raemakers, Théophile-Alexandre Steinlen, Achille Mauzan, Herbert Bayer and Leonetto Cappiello. However, we know comparatively little about other poster artists, many of whom worked in anonymity for governments or other agencies and have not received the recognition they are due.

The earlier campaigns show more use of negative motivators such as guilt and stigma: the father with his head in his hands sitting beside a young boy with polio under the slogan, "Why… Why didn't we listen?"; the moralizing messages about prostitutes and syphilis with slogans warning, "She may be a bag of trouble". But this approach gradually evolves towards more positive methods using humour, persuasion and involvement, rather than military-type direction. The anti-malaria campaign that recommends covering up reflects this more light-hearted approach; "Don't striptease for *Anopheles*", as does one for tobacco control; "Everyone loves a quitter – let's work together to be smoke-free".

All the posters are intended to persuade people to change their behaviour. But how do we know what really works? There has been no systematic collection or evaluation of massive social marketing campaigns and indeed this book presents only a smattering of the total global output on the subject. Posters vary hugely from country to country and over time. By publishing this book WHO hopes to spur those involved or interested in public health care campaigns to stop and think critically. Which posters work and which don't? How do we evaluate their effectiveness? Can a poster work on its own or does it need to be part of a much bigger approach to behavioural change? Although posters are getting flashier, are they getting better?

Good posters don't disappear, they tend to stick around and be used again. Beyond the images featured in this book, there is probably no public health problem which has not been tackled by a poster, for the medium is relatively inexpensive to develop and can be seen by people in a broad variety of settings. In developing countries where there are fewer competing media, the poster can make a big impact without costing too much. It is an effective means of getting an important message widely disseminated, and because of this public health posters have a valued past and a promising future.

Avant-propos

Il est difficile de dire ce qui fait passer le message sur une affiche. Comme pour tout moyen de propagande, le but est d'amener la personne qui voit l'affiche à adopter un comportement déterminé – acheter un produit dont on vante les mérites ou, dans le cas des affiches concernant la santé publique, modifier ou éliminer un comportement indésirable. Une affiche peut nous inciter à cesser de fumer, à nous faire vacciner, à utiliser le préservatif ou à ne pas échanger des seringues usagées. Il faut au moins qu'elle parvienne à retenir notre attention, ne serait-ce que pour quelques secondes, afin que nous puissions enregistrer le message qu'elle cherche à communiquer – un message qui prend souvent la forme d'une image saisissante, accompagnée de mots accrocheurs.

Alors que des messages de santé publique officiels étaient largement diffusés par les autorités locales et nationales, on utilisait rarement des affiches pour ces messages avant la première guerre mondiale. Mais à partir de 1917, alors qu'une grande partie du continent européen était à feu et à sang, les gouvernements ont jugé nécessaire de renforcer la santé et la résistance de la population. Ainsi, le Gouvernement français a réagi aux préoccupations concernant les ravages de l'alcoolisme, de la tuberculose et des maladies sexuellement transmissibles dans l'armée en lançant des campagnes de mise en garde destinées aux soldats. Les affiches ont joué un rôle important dans le cadre de cet effort. Les images frappantes et le ton souvent grinçant rappellent ceux de la propagande. Les affiches concernant la tuberculose préconisaient un traitement précoce, mettaient en garde contre les chambres mal aérées et lançaient des appels de fonds en faveur de la recherche.

Les artistes européens de premier plan qui ont travaillé pour des campagnes de santé publique sont bien connus et certaines de leurs œuvres sont représentées ici. Ainsi, les artistes français Lucien Lévy-Dhurmer et Jules-Abel Faivre ont placé la barre très haut pendant la première guerre mondiale et leur contribution résiste à l'épreuve du temps. Parmi les autres artistes renommés à qui l'on doit des affiches, on peut mentionner Ramón Casas, Franz von Stuck, Adolph Hohenstein, Louis Raemakers, Théophile-Alexandre Steinlen, Achille Mauzan, Herbert Bayer et Leonetto Cappiello. Mais nous savons assez peu de choses sur les autres artistes internationaux, dont beaucoup ont travaillé de façon anonyme pour les gouvernements ou d'autres organisations et dont la contribution n'a pas été reconnue à sa juste valeur.

Les campagnes les plus anciennes font davantage appel à des sentiments négatifs comme la culpabilité ou l'exclusion : le père effondré, la tête dans les mains assis à côté d'un jeune garçon paralysé par la poliomyélite, avec la légende « Mais pourquoi n'avons-nous pas écouté ? » en offre un bon exemple ; les messages moralisateurs sur les prostituées et la syphilis abondent avec, par exemple, la légende « Elle risque d'être une source de problèmes ». Mais cette approche a progressivement évolué avec l'adoption de conceptions plus positives faisant appel à l'humour, à la persuasion et à l'engagement plutôt qu'à des commandements de caractère militaire. C'est l'impression que peut donner la campagne de lutte antipaludique qui recommande d'éviter tout striptease face aux moustiques ou celle qui vante la popularité du fumeur qui abandonne la cigarette.

Toutes les affiches ont pour but d'amener les gens à modifier leur comportement, mais comment repérer celles qui y sont parvenues ? Il n'y a jamais eu d'évaluation, ni de collecte systématique des données sur les grandes campagnes de marketing social et le présent ouvrage ne contient qu'un petit échantillon de la production mondiale. Les affiches varient considérablement d'un pays à l'autre et d'une époque à l'autre. Par cette publication, l'OMS souhaite amener ceux qui participent à des campagnes de soins de santé publique ou qui s'y intéressent à réfléchir de manière critique au problème. Quelles sont les affiches qui « marchent » et celles qui ne marchent pas ? Comment pouvons-nous en évaluer le degré d'efficacité ? Une affiche peut-elle être prise isolément ou doit-elle s'insérer dans une approche plus large pour changer les comportements ? Les affiches deviennent certes plus accrocheuses, mais sont-elles meilleures pour autant ?

Une bonne affiche ne disparaît pas, elle a tendance à laisser son empreinte et à être réutilisée. Au-delà des illustrations dans les pages qui suivent, on aurait probablement du mal à trouver des problèmes de santé publique qui n'ont pas fait l'objet d'une affiche car il s'agit là d'un moyen relativement peu coûteux à mettre au point et pouvant être vu dans des cadres très différents. Dans les pays en développement où les médias concurrents sont rares, l'affiche peut avoir un impact considérable à moindre coût. Moyen efficace pour assurer une large diffusion à un message important de santé publique, l'affiche a joué un rôle crucial dans le passé et reste prometteuse pour l'avenir.

Prólogo

No es fácil identificar las claves de un cartel eficaz. Como cualquier otro medio de publicidad, los carteles se diseñan pensando en persuadir a quienes los vean para que hagan algo, ya sea comprar el producto anunciado o, en el caso de los carteles de salud pública, cambiar o suprimir hábitos nocivos. Un cartel puede pedirnos que dejemos de fumar, que nos vacunemos, que usemos preservativos o que no compartamos jeringas. Como mínimo, debe hacer que nos detengamos, siquiera sea unos segundos, para captar el mensaje, un mensaje que normalmente consiste en una imagen llamativa asociada a palabras contundentes.

Aunque los gobiernos locales y estatales venían recurriendo ampliamente a mensajes oficiales de salud pública, los carteles sobre esos temas eran escasos antes de la Primera Guerra Mundial. A partir de 1917, en una Europa asolada por la guerra, los gobiernos consideraron que era necesario potenciar la salud y las fuerzas de la población. Por ejemplo, en respuesta a la preocupación que causaban el alcoholismo, la tuberculosis y las enfermedades de transmisión sexual entre los militares, el Gobierno de Francia lanzó campañas públicas sostenidas para advertir de esos peligros. Los carteles fueron un componente esencial de esas iniciativas. Sus imágenes impactantes, unidas a menudo a un lenguaje estridente, imprimieron mayor fuerza de convicción a la propaganda. En los carteles sobre la tuberculosis se preconizaba el tratamiento precoz, se advertía que no se debía dormir con las ventanas cerradas y se pedían más fondos para investigación.

Aparecen en este libro algunos artistas europeos relevantes que diseñaron material para las campañas de salud pública. Así, la calidad de los trabajos alcanzó altas cotas con los franceses Lucien Lévy-Dhurmer y Abel Faivre, cuya obra, en consecuencia, no acusa el paso del tiempo. Otros cartelistas famosos son Ramón Casas, Franz Van Stock, Adolph Hohenstein, Louis Raemakers, Théophile-Alexandre Steinlen, Achille Mauzan, Herbert Bayer y Leonetto Cappiello. Sin embargo, sabemos relativamente poco sobre otros artistas internacionales, muchos de los cuales trabajaron de forma anónima para gobiernos y organismos y no han recibido el reconocimiento que se merecen.

En las primeras campañas se observa un mayor uso de factores motivadores negativos, como la culpa y la estigmatización; por ejemplo ese padre sentado junto al niño con poliomielitis, que se pregunta abatido "¿Por qué? ¿Por qué no hicimos caso?", o los mensajes moralizantes sobre las prostitutas y la sífilis, con lemas que advertían que "Esta mujer puede ser un foco de problemas". Pero ese enfoque se vio reemplazado gradualmente por otras técnicas más positivas basadas en el humor, la persuasión y la participación, más que en la coacción de tinte militar. La campaña contra la malaria que recomienda cubrirse refleja esa mayor frescura de los mensajes, por ejemplo "No se desnude ante Anofeles", como se observa también en una campaña contra el tabaco: «Todos te querrán si lo dejas - Unámonos para eliminar el humo».

Todos los carteles tienden a persuadir a la gente para que modifique su comportamiento, pero ¿cómo podemos saber si son realmente eficaces? No se ha hecho ningún acopio ni evaluación sistemáticos de las campañas masivas de mercadotecnia social, y de hecho en este libro se ofrece sólo un atisbo de todo lo publicado a nivel mundial sobre el tema. Los carteles varían mucho de un país a otro y a lo largo del tiempo. Publicando esta obra, la OMS espera estimular a todos los implicados o interesados en las campañas de salud pública para que hagan una pausa y piensen críticamente. ¿Qué carteles funcionan y cuáles no? ¿Cómo podemos evaluar su eficacia? ¿Puede un cartel influir por sí solo, o es necesario enmarcarlo en una operación mucho más amplia de fomento de cambios comportamentales? Además de ser cada vez más llamativos, ¿son los carteles también cada vez mejores?

Los buenos carteles, lejos de desaparecer, acaban volviendo a ser utilizados. Al margen de las imágenes presentadas en este libro, probablemente no hay ningún problema de salud pública que no haya sido abordado con un cartel, dado que se trata de un medio relativamente barato y que la gente puede ver en muy diversas circunstancias. En los países en desarrollo, donde hay menos medios que le hagan competencia, un cartel puede tener gran impacto sin un costo excesivo. Por ello, porque son una alternativa eficaz para difundir ampliamente mensajes importantes, los carteles de salud pública tienen un pasado valioso y un futuro prometedor.

Предисловие

Определение того, что делает плакат эффективным, является трудным вопросом. Подобно любому пропагандистскому материалу, он предназначен для того, чтобы убедить зрителя в необходимости что-то сделать - либо купить рекламируемое изделие, либо, в случае плаката на тему общественного здравоохранения, изменить или ликвидировать разрушительные привычки. Плакат может призывать нас бросить курить, вакцинироваться, использовать презервативы или не пользоваться общими иглами. Самое меньшее, он должен заставить нас остановиться, хотя бы на несколько секунд, чтобы воспринять содержащееся в нем сообщение - сообщение, которое обычно принимает форму действенного изображения, сопровождаемого убедительными словами.

Несмотря на широкое использование официальных сообщений общественного здравоохранения местными и национальными органами, реальные плакаты на эту тему до Первой мировой войны практические отсутствовали. Начиная с 1917 г., когда сражения охватили всю Европу, правительства почувствовали необходимость в энергичном укреплении здоровья населения. Например, Французское правительство отреагировало на обеспокоенность относительно алкоголизма, туберкулеза и болезней, передаваемых половым путем, среди военнослужащих, посредством создания постоянных кампаний информирования об этих опасностях. Плакаты были неотъемлемой частью этих усилий. Их броские изображения и часто жесткие формулировки создали общую обстановку активной пропаганды. Плакаты про туберкулез пропагандировали раннее лечение, предупреждали о необходимости спать с открытыми окнами и призывали выделить больше средств на исследования.

Выдающиеся европейские художники, которые создавшие рисунки для кампаний общественного здравоохранения, хорошо известны и некоторые из них упоминаются в этой книге. Например, французские художники Люсьен Леви-Дурмер и Абель Февр установили высокие стандарты во время Первой мировой войны и в результате их работа приобрела непреходящую ценность. Другие известные художники плакатов включают Рамона Казаса, Франца Ван Стока, Адольфа Хохенстайна, Луи Ремейкерса, Теофила-Александра Стейнлина, Ахилла Мозана, Герберта Байера и Леонетто Каппиелло. Вместе с тем, мы знаем относительно немного о других международных художниках, многие из которых работали анонимно для правительств или других учреждений и не получили должного признания.

В ходе ранних кампаний больше использовались негативные факторы мотивации, такие как чувство вины и клеймо позора: отец, охвативший руками голову и сидящий позади мальчика с полиомиелитом под такими словами: "Почему… почему мы не слушали раньше?"; морализирующее сообщение о проститутках и сифилисе с предупреждающей надписью: "Она может быть источником неприятностей". Однако этот подход постепенно изменился в сторону более позитивных методов, использующих юмор, убеждение и участие, а не военные методы. Кампания борьбы с малярией, которая рекомендует накрываться, отражает этот более легкий подход: "Не раздевайся перед комарами", так же как и текст, используемый для борьбы против табака: "Все любят тех, кто бросил курить, давайте работать вместе, чтобы создать бездымную среду".

Все плакаты предназначены для того, чтобы убедить людей изменить свое поведение, но как мы узнаем, что действительно воздействует? До сих пор не было систематической подборки или оценки массовых кампаний социального маркетинга и в этой книге, действительно, представлен лишь поверхностный взгляд на общие глобальные результаты в этом вопросе. Плакаты всегда очень сильно отличались в зависимости от страны и времени. Публикуя эту книгу, ВОЗ надеется заставить тех, кто участвует в кампаниях общественного здравоохранения или заинтересован в таких кампаниях, остановиться и критически взглянуть на вещи. Какие плакаты действуют, а какие нет? Как мы оцениваем их эффективность? Может ли плакат воздействовать самостоятельно или он должен быть частью гораздо более широкого подхода к изменению поведения? Хотя плакаты становятся более заметными, становятся ли они лучше?

Хорошие плакаты не исчезают, они остаются надолго и используются вновь. Помимо изображений, представленных в этой книге, вероятно, нет такой проблемы общественного здравоохранения, которая не была бы изображена с помощью плаката, - средства, которое относительно недорого сделать и которое люди могут увидеть в самых разнообразных местах. В развивающихся странах, где существует меньше конкурирующих средств массовой информации, плакат может оказать сильное воздействие без слишком больших расходов. Он является эффективным средством широкого распространения важного сообщения и именно поэтому плакаты на тему общественного здравоохранения ценились в прошлом и имеют обещающее будущее.

前言

要确定海报的有效性，并不是一件容易的事。就像任何宣传品一样，设计海报是用来说服观众做事的，或者期望购买所宣传的产品，或者就公共卫生方面的海报而言，期望纠正或者消除不良习惯。海报可能会恳请人们戒烟、接种疫苗、使用避孕套或不要共用针具。海报至少会使我们驻足观看（哪怕仅有几秒钟），了解其主题内容。主题内容的表达形式往往是有说服力的图像，加上有力的言辞。

尽管地方和国家政府广泛使用了官方公共卫生信息，第一次世界大战之前关于此类主题的真正海报寥寥无几。1917年，战争开始席卷了整个欧洲，从此以后，国家政府感到，有必要强化公众健康和体力。举例来说，法国政府针对一些关注的问题采取了应对行动，通过创立持续性公共宣传活动，告诫军人由酗酒、患结核病和性病带来的危险。海报就是这方面工作的组成部分，其突出的外观和常常刺目的言辞引领出一种格调有力的宣传方式。结核病的海报宣扬了早期治疗，告诫人们不要开窗睡觉，并且呼吁投入更多的研究资金。

为公共卫生活动进行构思创作的，不乏欧洲知名的突出艺术家。他们中有些在本书中有突出介绍。比如，法国艺术家Lucien Lévy-Dhurmer及 Abel Faivre在第一次世界大战期间就订立了高标准，结果使其作品亘古永存。其他著名的艺术家还有 Ramón Casas, Franz Van Stock, Adolph Hohenstein, Louis Raemakers, Théophile-Alexandre Steinlen, Achille Mauzan, Herbert Bayer 以及Leonetto Cappiello。但是，相比而言，我们对其他的国际艺术家知之甚少，他们中的很多人为政府或其他机构默默无闻地工作，而没有得到应有的认可。

早期的宣传活动更多利用反面因素作为行动的动力，如内疚和耻辱。一位父亲双手托着脑袋，旁边坐着一位患有小儿麻痹的幼儿，宣传口号为：'为什么--为什么我们不听？'；在对妓女和梅毒问题进行训戒时，警告宣传口号是："她可能会带来一大堆麻烦"。但是，这样的宣传方式逐渐向更加积极的方向转变，改用了幽默、说服和参与的方法，而不是使用军事命令的方式。在控制疟疾宣传活动中，建议人们穿严衣服，反映出所采用的是一种轻松自然的宣传方式：'不要袒露肢体，惹按蚊叮咬'。烟草控制也是一样：'所有人都喜爱戒烟者一携手工作，放弃烟草'。

从本意上看，所有海报都是劝说人们改变行为的。可是，我们怎样知道是什么在发挥作用？至今为止，还没有对大型社会宣传活动进行过系统的收集或评价。这本书确实只是这方面所有全球作品的一瞥。国与国之间，以及随着时间变迁，海报差异很大。世卫组织出版这本书，希望那些参与或热衷于公共卫生保健活动的人们得到鞭策，暂时放下手中的工作，审慎地思考一番。到底怎样的海报起作用，怎样的不起作用？怎样评价其有效性？海报可以独立发挥作用，还是需要成为较大行为改变方式的组成部分？尽管海报越来越俗丽，可它是否越来越受欢迎呢？

好的海报不会消失，它会流传下去，并会再次使用。在本书特载的图像之外，可能找不到哪一个公共卫生问题从未使用过海报。这是因为这种手段制作起来相对廉价，并且可为背景各异的人们所看到。就发展中国家而言，具有竞争力的媒体较少，海报花费不多，但成效很大。海报是广泛传播重要主题内容的有效方式。正是因为如此，公共卫生海报过去受到过珍视，未来前途光明。

توطئة

إن تحديد ما يحققه الملصق الإعلاني الذي يتم إعداده بإتقان ليس بالمسألة السهلة. وعلى غرار أي مادة دعائية يتم تصميم الملصق الإعلاني بحيث يقنع المشاهد بعمل شيء ما، كشراء المنتج المعلن عنه أو تغيير عادات هدامة أو الإقلاع عنها في حالة الملصقات الإعلانية الخاصة بالصحة العمومية. وقد يناشدنا الملصق الإعلاني الإقلاع عن التدخين أو أخذ اللقاح أو استعمال العازل الذكري أو عدم تبادل الإبر. ويجب، على أقل تقدير، أن يجعلنا نتوقف ولو لبضع ثوان فحسب من أجل استيعاب الرسالة، وهي رسالة تأخذ عادة شكل صورة مؤثرة مصحوبة بعبارات طنانة.

وعلى الرغم من استعمال رسائل الصحة العمومية الرسمية على نطاق واسع من قِبَل الحكومات المحلية وحكومات الولايات كان من النادر قبل الحرب العالمية الأولى إعداد ملصقات إعلانية بشأن هذه المواضيع بالفعل. وابتداءً من عام 1917، وبينما كانت المعارك تعصف بجميع أنحاء أوروبا، استشعرت الحكومات أن من الضروري الاستجابة للهواجس ذات الصلة. وعلى سبيل المثال استجابت الحكومة الفرنسية للهواجس ذات الصلة بإدمان الكحول والسل والأمراض المنقولة جنسياً بين المجندين فدشنت حملات عمومية مستديمة للتحذير من هذه الأخطار. وكان إعداد الملصقات الإعلانية جزءاً لا يتجزأ من هذه الجهود. وبفضل شكلها الآخذ ولغتها الرنانة عادة تحقق شكل من أشكال الدعاية الفعالة. ودعت الملصقات الإعلانية الخاصة بالسل إلى العلاج المبكر وحذرت من الخلود إلى النوم وجميع النوافذ مغلقة وطالبت برصد المزيد من الأموال للبحوث.

وقد وضعت التصاميم الخاصة بحملات الصحة العمومية على يد فنانين أوروبيين بارزين ومشاهير، وقد تم تسليط الضوء على بعضهم في هذا الكتاب. فعلى سبيل المثال التزم الفنانان الفرنسيان لوسيان ليفي- درمر وآبل فيفر بمعايير عالية أثناء الحرب العالمية الأولى ومن ثم فقد كتب الخلود لأعمالهم الفنية. ومن بين الفنانين المشاهير الآخرين الذين صمموا الملصقات الإعلانية رامون كازاز وفرانز فان ستوك وأدولف أوهنشتين ولويس ريمكرز وتيوفيل- ألكسندر ستنلن وأشيل موزان

وهيربيرت باير وليونيتو كابيلو. ومع ذلك فنحن لا نعرف إلا القليل نسبياً عن فنانين دوليين آخرين، عمل كثير منهم دون ذكر اسمه في حكومات أو في وكالات أخرى ما، ولم يحظوا بالتقدير الواجب.

وشهدت الحملات الأولى استخداماً أكبر لمثبطات، مثل الشعور بالذنب والوصم: ومن أمثلة ذلك صورة الأب الذي يضع رأسه بين يديه ويجلس بجوار صبي صغير مصاب بشلل الأطفال تحت شعار «لماذا... لماذا لم نصغِ؟»؛ والرسائل التي تحض على الأخلاق والمتعلقة بالعاهرات والزهري تحت شعار تحذيري هو «إنها قد تكون مصيبة بجلاجل». بيد أن هذا الأسلوب لم يلبث أن تطور بالتدريج إلى أساليب أكثر إيجابية تستخدم الدعابة والإقناع والإشراك بدلاً من التعليمات الأقرب إلى التوجيهات العسكرية. وقد اختارت حملة مكافحة الملاريا التي توصي بالتغطية هذا الأسلوب الأقرب إلى المرح تحت شعار مثل «لا تترك نفسك عارياً وعرضة لبعوض الأنوفيلة»، وهو الأسلوب الذي اتبع أيضاً في مكافحة التبغ بشعار مثل «الكل يحب من ينجح في الامتناع - لنعمل معا على التحرر من التدخين».

وقد أعدت جميع الملصقات الإعلانية من أجل إقناع الناس بتغيير سلوكهم، ولكن كيف لنا أن نعرف الملصقات الإعلانية التي تحقق هدفها بالفعل؟ ولم يتم بصورة منهجية تقصي أو تقييم حملات التسويق الاجتماعي الضخمة، ولا يعرض هذا الكتاب بالفعل إلا نظرة عامة على مجموع الحصائل العالمية الخاصة بهذه المسألة. وتختلف الملصقات الإعلانية اختلافا هائلا من بلد إلى آخر ومن عصر إلى عصر. وتأمل المنظمة، بنشرها هذا الكتاب، في حفز المشاركين في حملات رعاية الصحة العمومية أو المهتمين بها على التوقف والتفكير النقدي في الأمر. فما هي الملصقات الإعلانية التي تحقق هدفها وما هي الملصقات الإعلانية التي لا تحقق هدفها؟ وكيف لنا أن نقيم فعاليتها؟ وهل يمكن للملصق الإعلاني أن يحقق هدفه بمفرده أم يلزم أن يكون جزءاً من أسلوب أوسع نطاقا يستهدف تغيير السلوك؟ وعلى الرغم من أن الملصقات الإعلانية تزداد بهرجة أكثر فأكثر فإن لنا أن نسأل هل هي في تحسن أم لا؟

Vaccinate. Vaccination is widely acclaimed as one of the world's most effective public health interventions. Global immunization programmes have brought nine major diseases under varying degrees of control and the campaign posters in this chapter track the history vividly.

The story begins in the 1950s when the Salk polio vaccine had a miraculous impact on the ravaging epidemics current at the time. In 1966, WHO and the Centers for Disease Control began the worldwide smallpox eradication campaign in Africa, followed by similar initiatives in Asia up to 1979, when the world was finally declared smallpox free.

To increase the dismal 5% of children in developing countries who were being reached by immunization services for other diseases, WHO set up the Expanded Programme on Immunization (EPI) in 1974 to provide the following vaccies: Bacillus Calmette-Guerin (BCG), diphtheria-tetanus-pertussis (DTP), oral poliovirus vaccine, and measles vaccine. The combined measles, mumps and rubella vaccination was added later in industrialized countries.

Increasingly, approaches shifted towards integrating immunization for children and pregnant women with routine primary health care services, accompanied by massive staff training and communication efforts. Posters from this period are much more informative than the earlier ones, giving parents details of the expected immunization schedule and encouraging the use of vaccination cards.

Although EPI increased coverage rates, pockets of low access and refusal persisted. In the 1990s, many countries established national immunization programmes. These linked routine immunization with targeted national days focused on particular diseases, in which brigades of vaccinators would often move house-to-house.

Poster images have shifted in relation to these changing vaccination priorities and approaches, and have responded to broader social and cultural trends. Those of the 1950s play on fear, showing the devastating effects of polio with images of damaged children and parents. In contrast, the concerted, optimistic campaigns of the smallpox eradication period portray vaccination as a fight, exhorting people to join. Education campaigns at this time were often one-way, telling people what to do. By the late 1970s such military-style images give way to those of holding, shielding and embracing – symbolized by hands and umbrellas, for instance – perhaps more in line with emerging cultural understandings of health protection and of the immune system. Vaccinated children are presented as healthy, smiling and busy. Other images appeal to parental responsibility, equating the good parent with someone who completes the schedule and enables their child to flourish.

Vacciner. La vaccination est largement considérée comme l'une des interventions de santé publique mondiale les plus efficaces. Les programmes de vaccination mondiaux ont permis de maîtriser plus ou moins parfaitement neuf grandes maladies et les affiches dans ce chapitre retracent leur utilisation de manière saisissante.

L'histoire commence pendant les années 50 lorsque le vaccin antipoliomyélitique Salk a eu un effet miraculeux contre les épidémies de poliomyélite qui faisaient rage. En 1966, l'OMS et les Centers for Disease Control ont lancé la campagne mondiale d'éradication de la variole en Afrique, suivie d'initiatives semblables en Asie jusqu'en 1979 quand le monde a finalement été déclaré libéré du fléau.

En 1974, alors que les services de vaccination contre d'autres maladies ne parvenaient qu'à protéger 5 % des enfants des pays en développement, l'OMS a créé le Programme élargi de Vaccination (PEV); il fournira le BCG (Bacille de Calmette et de Guérin), le DTCoq (diphtérie-tétanos-coqueluche), le vaccin oral contre la poliomyélite et le vaccin anti-rougeoleux. Le vaccin trivalent contre la rougeole, les oreillons et la rubéole a été rajouté par la suite dans les pays industrialisés.

Progressivement, on a cherché à intégrer la vaccination de l'enfant et de la femme enceinte dans le cadre des services de soins de santé primaires systématiques, avec un effort massif de formation et de communication. Les affiches de cette période fournissent davantage d'informations que les précédentes, donnant aux parents des précisions sur le calendrier vaccinal et encourageant l'utilisation des carnets de vaccination.

Si le programme élargi a permis d'améliorer les taux de couverture, des poches de non-vaccinés ont subsisté en raison des difficultés d'accès à certaines zones ou de la méfiance communautaire. Au cours des années 90, de nombreux pays ont mis sur pied des programmes nationaux de vaccination reliant la vaccination systématique à des journées nationales consacrées à des maladies déterminées, au cours desquelles de nombreux agents de vaccination faisaient souvent du porte à porte.

Les affiches ont évolué parallèlement à la modification des priorités et des approches en matière de vaccination et à la prise en compte de tendances socioculturelles plus larges. Celles des années 50 mettent l'accent sur la crainte, montrant les effets dévastateurs de la poliomyélite avec des illustrations d'enfants paralysés et de leurs parents effondrés. Au contraire, les campagnes concertées et optimistes aboutissant à l'éradication de la variole dépeignent la vaccination comme un combat auquel les gens sont invités à se joindre. Les campagnes d'éducation à cette époque allaient souvent en sens unique, se bornant à indiquer aux gens ce qu'il fallait faire. Dès la fin des années 70, ce « militarisme » a disparu et l'on a cherché à soutenir, protéger ou entourer, en ayant recours à des symboles comme les mains et les parapluies, avec des illustrations correspondant davantage aux perceptions culturelles naissantes de la protection de la santé et du système immunitaire. L'enfant vacciné apparaît comme souriant, actif et en bonne santé. D'autres illustrations font appel à la responsabilité parentale, le bon comportement consistant à veiller au respect scrupuleux du calendrier vaccinal et à l'épanouissement de l'enfant.

■ **Vacunar.** La vacunación goza de un amplio reconocimiento como una de las intervenciones más eficaces de salud pública en todo el mundo. Los programas mundiales de inmunización han permitido controlar en mayor o menor medida nueve importantes enfermedades, y los carteles de campañas presentados en este capítulo ilustran gráficamente esos logros.

La historia comienza en los años cincuenta, cuando la vacuna antipoliomielítica de Salk tuvo un impacto milagroso en la epidemia de esa enfermedad, que por entonces hacía estragos en la población. En 1966, la OMS y los Centros para el Control de Enfermedades iniciaron la campaña mundial de erradicación de la viruela en África, a lo que siguieron iniciativas similares en Asia hasta 1979, año en que por fin pudo declararse que el mundo se había liberado de la poliomielitis.

A fin de aumentar el deplorable porcentaje del 5% de los niños de los países en desarrollo a los que llegaban los servicios de inmunización para otras enfermedades, la OMS creó en 1974 el Programa Ampliado de Inmunización (PAI) en cuyo marco se proporcionaron las vacunas siguientes: contra el bacilo Calmette-Guérin (BCG), contra la difteria, el tétanos y la tos ferina (DTP), la vacuna antipoliomielítica oral, y la vacuna antitetánica. Más tarde se añadió en los países industrializados la vacunación combinada contra el sarampión, la parotiditis y la rubéola.

Las estrategias seguidas evolucionaron cada vez más por la senda de la integración de la inmunización de los niños y las mujeres embarazadas en los servicios de atención primaria habituales, unida a esfuerzos masivos de formación del personal y de comunicación. Los carteles de ese periodo, mucho más informativos que los anteriores, detallaban para los padres el calendario de inmunización previsto y alentaban a emplear las cartillas de vacunación.

Aunque el PAI aumentó las tasas de cobertura, persistían las bolsas de bajo acceso y de rechazo. En los años noventa, numerosos países establecieron programas nacionales de inmunización. Con ellos la inmunización sistemática se vinculó a días nacionales centrados en determinadas enfermedades, en los que brigadas de vacunadores hacían rondas casa por casa.

Las imágenes de los carteles han evolucionado a la par que las sucesivas prioridades y estrategias de vacunación, respondiendo a tendencias sociales y culturales más generales. Las de los años cincuenta recurren al miedo, mostrando los devastadores efectos de la poliomielitis con imágenes de niños y padres afectados. Contrastando con ello, las campañas coordinadas y optimistas del periodo de erradicación de la viruela muestran la vacunación como una lucha y exhortan a la gente a unirse a ella. Las campañas de educación de la época eran a menudo unidireccionales, limitándose a decirle a la población lo que tenía que hacer. A finales de los años setenta esas imágenes militares dan paso a otras que connotan protección y apoyo, como por ejemplo manos y paraguas, más en consonancia quizá con los mayores conocimientos sobre la protección sanitaria y el sistema inmunitario. Los niños vacunados se presentan con aspecto sano, sonrientes y activos. Otras imágenes apelan a la responsabilidad de los padres, elogiando a los que completan el calendario de vacunación y permiten así que su hijo crezca saludablemente.

■ **Вакцинируйтесь.** Вакцинация широко пропагандируется как одно из самых эффективных мероприятий общественного здравоохранения в мире.

Глобальные программы иммунизации в различной степени поставили под контроль девять основных болезней, и плакаты этих кампаний, представленные в настоящей главе, ярко отражают историю.

История начинается в 1950-х годах, когда вакцина Солка против полиомиелита оказала чудодейственное воздействие на опустошительные эпидемии, происходившие в то время. В 1966 г. ВОЗ и Центры борьбы с болезнями начали всемирную кампанию по ликвидации оспы в Африке, вслед за которой была предпринята подобная инициатива в Азии, продолжавшаяся до 1979 г., когда мир окончательно был провозглашен свободным от полиомиелита.

Для увеличения катастрофической цифры в 5% детей в развивающихся странах, охваченных службами иммунизации против других болезней, в 1974 г. ВОЗ создала расширенную программу иммунизации (РПИ) для предоставления следующих вакцин: БЦЖ (бацилла Кальметта-Герина), АКДС (коклюш-дифтерия-столбняк), пероральная полиовирусная вакцина и противокоревая вакцина. Позднее в промышленно развитых странах была добавлена комбинированная вакцинация против кори, эпидемического паротита и краснухи.

Применяемые подходы все больше изменялись в сторону интеграции иммунизации детей и беременных женщин в регулярные службы первичной медико-санитарной помощи, что сопровождалось массовой подготовкой персонала и усилиями по распространению информации. Плакаты этого периода являются гораздо более информативными, чем прежде, предоставляя детальную информацию для родителей о предполагаемых графиках иммунизации и поощряя использовать карточки вакцинации.

Несмотря на то, что РПИ увеличила степень охвата, отдельные очаги низкого доступа и отказа продолжали существовать. В 1990-е годы многие страны создали национальные программы иммунизации. Они связали регулярную иммунизацию с целевыми национальными днями, сосредоточенными на конкретных болезнях, в ходе которых бригады вакцинаторов часто ходили от дома к дому.

Изображения на плакатах изменялись в зависимости от изменяющихся приоритетов и подходов к вакцинации и реагировали на более широкие социальные и культурные тенденции. Плакаты 1950-х годов воздействовали на страх, показывая разрушительное воздействие полиомиелита с помощью изображения пострадавших детей и родителей. В отличие от этого, согласованные, оптимистические кампании периода ликвидации оспы отражали вакцинацию как борьбу, призывая людей присоединиться к этой борьбе. Просветительские кампании в это время часто были односторонними, говоря людям, что делать. К концу 1970-х годов такие изображения военного образца уступили место изображениям с идеями охраны, защиты и охвата, символизируемыми, например, руками и зонтиками, которые, вероятно, больше соответствовали возникающим культурным идеям охраны здоровья и иммунной системы. Вакцинированные дети представлялись здоровыми, улыбающимися и играющими. Другие изображения призывали родителей к ответственности, приравнивая хороших родителей к тем, кто выполняет графики иммунизации и обеспечивает процветание своих детей.

■ **疫苗接种。**疫苗接种是世界上最有效的公共卫生干预措施之一，得到了广泛赞誉。全球计划免疫规划的创立使得九种主要传染病得到了不同程度的控制。本章节介绍的活动海报生动地记录了这个历史。

这段历史情况始于50年代，当时脊灰流行带来了破坏性影响，索尔克脊灰疫苗具有神奇的作用。1966年，世卫组织和美国疾病控制和预防中心在非洲启动了全球消除天花活动，随后在亚洲也采取了类似行动，直到1979年全世界最终宣布没有天花为止。

为使发展中国家获得计划免疫服务的5%不幸儿童更多地得到其它疾病的免疫保护，世卫组织于1974年设立了扩大免疫规划，提供下列疫苗：卡介苗、白百破三联疫苗、口服脊灰疫苗以及麻疹疫苗。工业化国家后来增加了麻疹、腮腺炎和风疹联合免疫。

所采取的方式越来越多地发生了转变，目标是将儿童和孕妇计划免疫与初级卫生保健常规服务相结合，同时伴有大量人员培训和宣传活动。从这时起，海报与以往相比信息量更大，不仅向父母介绍选定的计划免疫接种程序的细节，还鼓励使用接种卡。

尽管扩大免疫规划使得接种覆盖率得以提高，但是仍然存在获得性不够及拒绝接种的散在情况。在90年代，许多国家设立了国家免疫规划。这些相互关联并且具有特定国家日的计划免疫活动，重点解决特定的疾病，每当这时，接种人员小分队常常挨家挨户走动。

随着免疫接种重点和方式的变化，海报的图像发生了转变，并且针对更加广泛的社会和文化趋势作出了反应。50年代的海报图像利用了恐惧感，以受影响的儿童和父母图像展现脊灰带来的蹂躏。相比较而言，在消除天花时期，一些齐心协力和乐观主义的宣传活动则将计划免疫表现为一场战斗，恳劝人们参与进来。此时的宣教活动通常是单向的，也就是告知人们该做什么。到了70年代后期，此类军事化性质的图像被托住、防护和拥抱性的图像所取代（比如，用手和雨伞作为象征），这可能与当时对健康保护和免疫系统的新兴文化理解较为一致。获得接种的儿童被表现为健康向上、笑容满面，并且无休止地活动。有的图像恳请父母担起责任，也就是将好的父母等同于哪些完成免疫程序并使孩子健康成长的人们。

عليكم بالتطعيم. يحظى التطعيم بالتقدير على نطاق واسع باعتباره من أفعل تدخلات الصحة العمومية في العالم. وقد وضعت برامج التمنيع العالمية تسعة من أهم الأمراض تحت درجات مختلفة من السيطرة، وملصقات الحملة الإعلانية المعروضة في هذا الفصل تتتبع هذا التاريخ بنشاط.

وقد بدأت القصة في الخمسينيات من القرن العشرين عندما حقق لقاح شلل الأطفال المسمى «سالك» أثراً رائعاً في دحر الأوبئة التي استشرت إبان ذاك. وفي عام 1966 بدأت منظمة الصحة العالمية ومراكز مكافحة الأمراض الحملة العالمية لاستئصال الجدري في أفريقيا ثم استهلت مبادرات مماثلة في آسيا حتى عام 1979 عندما أعلن في خاتمة المطاف خلو العالم من الجدري.

وفي عام 1974 أنشأت المنظمة البرنامج الموسع للتمنيع كي تزيد نسبة الأطفال الهزيلة البالغة 5% التي تصل إليها خدمات التمنيع ضد الأمراض الأخرى في البلدان النامية. وذلك لتوفير اللقاحات التالية: البي سي جي واللقاح الثلاثي ضد الخناق والكزاز والشاهوق ولقاح شلل الأطفال الفموي ولقاح الحصبة وبعد ذلك أضيف في البلدان الصناعية اللقاح المؤلف ضد الحصبة والنكاف والحصبة الألمانية.

وتحولت الأساليب المتبعة أكثر فأكثر نحو التمنيع المتكامل للأطفال والحوامل بواسطة خدمات الرعاية الصحية الأولية الروتينية المصحوبة بجهود ضخمة في مجالي تدريب العاملين والاتصال.

وكانت الملصقات الإعلانية المستخدمة في هذه الحقبة أكثر توعية بكثير من سابقاتها، حيث كانت تزود الوالدين بمعلومات مفصلة عن جدول التمنيع المتوقع وتشجع على استخدام بطاقات التطعيم.

وعلى الرغم من أن البرنامج الموسع زاد معدلات التغطية فقد ظلت هناك مناطق يقل الوصول إليها ويرفض أهلها التمنيع. وفي التسعينيات من القرن العشرين أنشأت بلدان عديدة برامج تمنيع وطنية. وقد ربطت هذه البرامج التمنيع بأيام وطنية محددة تركز على أمراض معينة وكان غالباً ما ينتقل فيها أفراد فرق التطعيم من منزل إلى منزل.

وطرأت تغيرات على صور الملصقات الإعلانية في ما يتعلق بأولويات وأساليب التطعيم المتغيرة تلك، وتجاوبت مع ميول اجتماعية وثقافية أعم. وقد عزفت صور الملصقات الإعلانية في الخمسينات من القرن العشرين على وتر الخوف، حيث كانت تبين الآثار المدمرة لشلل الأطفال والآباء الذين لحق بهم الأذى. وعلى النقيض من ذلك فإن الحقبة التي شهدت حملات استئصال الجدري والمتفائلة صورت التطعيم على أنه كفاح تحض الناس على الانضمام إليه. واتخذت حملات التوعية إبان ذاك اتجاهاً واحداً، ألا وهو إخبار الناس بما يتعين عليهم أن يفعلوه. وبحلول أواخر السبعينات من القرن العشرين غابت هذه الصور الأقرب إلى الطابع العسكري لتحل محلها صور الاحتواء والحماية والعناق، التي عبرت عنها صور الأيدي والمظلات على سبيل المثال، وربما كان ذلك أكثر تماشياً مع الفهم الثقافي المستجد لحماية الصحة ونظام المناعة. وبرزت صورة الأطفال المطعمين كأطفال أصحاء ترتسم البسمة على شفاههم وينهمكون في الأنشطة. وكانت هناك صور أخرى تهيب بالوالدين أن يتحملا مسؤوليتهما، وتصور الأب الجيد على أنه الأب الذي يُتم جدول التمنيع ويمكّن أطفاله من النمو والترعرع.

الأستاذة ميليسا ليتش، مركز الطرق الاجتماعية والتكنولوجية والبيئية للاستدامة، معهد الدراسات الإنمائية، جامعة ساسيكس، برايتون، إنكلترا.

Why...Why Didn't We Listen?

Effective as it is, polio vaccine helps only when used.

Polio virus is still widespread.

Don't wait until it's too late. Arrange now for immunization.

Your pharmacist ℞ works for better community health.

CAMPAGNE CONTRE LA VARIOLE ET LA ROUGEOLE

Guyessi bi Kangha Sŭr Sen nom toto,
Nyamb Săn n'dat n'yi wa nyën
Bi y Kit-eb bagh yan.
Nyamb Kŭlem la y Kyelem bé boghben wăn.

Ayi din ni filè

A Djoussou Kadi
Aka la dégué: Ayi Tiriri la
Sini Kama !

VACCINEZ VOS ENFANTS

Regardez cet enfant, il est heureux.

Comme lui, faites-vous vacciner.

Votre avenir en dépend.

MINISTERE DE LA SANTE, DE LA POPULATION ET DES AFFAIRES SOCIALES / USAID

■ Mais pourquoi n'avons-nous pas écouté ? Le vaccin contre la poliomyélite est efficace, mais encore faut-il l'utiliser. Le poliovirus est encore répandu. Agissez avant qu'il ne soit trop tard. Faites-vous vacciner dès maintenant. ■ ¿Por qué ? ¿Por qué no hicimos caso? La vacuna antipoliomielítica es eficaz, pero sólo si se administra a tiempo. El poliovirus sigue muy extendido. No espere hasta que sea demasiado tarde. Pida ya su cita de vacunación. ■ Почему, … почему мы не слушали? Такая эффективная вакцина против полиомиелита помогает только тогда, когда ее принимают. А вирус полиомиелита все еще распространен. Не ждите, когда будет слишком поздно. Договоритесь уже сейчас об иммунизации. ■ 为什么—为什么我们不听？脊灰疫苗很有效，使用之后有好处。脊灰病毒无处不在，不要等到为时已晚。现在就准备接种疫苗。

■ لماذا؟ لماذا نحن لا نصغي؟ لقاح شلل الأطفال بفعاليته تلك ليست له أي فائدة إذا لم يستعمل. وفيروس شلل الأطفال مازال واسع الانتشار. لا تنتظر إلى أن يفوت الوقت. وعليك من الآن أن ترتب للتمنيع.

■ Campaign against smallpox and measles. ■ Campaña contra la viruela y el sarampión. ■ Кампания по борьбе против оспы и кори. ■ 控制水痘和麻疹运动。

■ حملة مكافحة الجدري والحصبة.

■ Tetanus: a threat to all. Vaccine: protection for each of us.
■ El tétanos: un peligro para todos. Con la vacuna estamos protegidos. ■ Столбняк представляет опасность для всех, а вакцина – защиту для каждого. ■ 破伤风：危及所有人。疫苗：保护我们每个人。

■ التيتانوس خطر على الجميع واللقاح حماية للجميع.

■ 10 June, vaccination against infant paralysis.
■ Le 10 juin, vaccination contre la paralysie infantile.
■ El 10 de junio, vacunación contra la parálisis infantil.
■ 10 июня – день вакцинации против детского паралича.
■ 6月10日：接种疫苗，预防婴儿瘫痪。

■ التطعيم ضد شلل الأطفال.

Recompensa – $1000. ■ Вознаграждение в 1000 долл.
奖赏--1000美元。

التطالتطعيم ضد شلل الأطفال. ■

Variole. Le point de non-retour. ■ La viruela. Punto sin retorno.
■ Оспа. Только вперед, назад возврата нет. ■ 天花：到了无法卷土
重来时刻。

الجدري. نقطة اللاعودة. ■

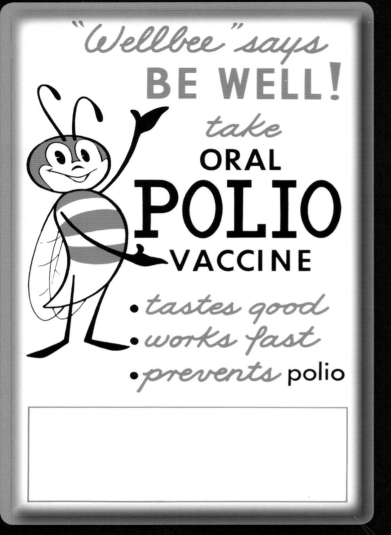

■ Protégez votre famille contre la poliomyélite et les autres maladies graves. ■ Proteja a su familia contra la poliomielitis y otras enfermedades temibles. ■ Защити свою семью от полиомиелита и других страшных болезней. ■ 保护你的家庭，防范脊灰和其它凶疾威胁。
■ عليك بحماية أسرتك من شلل الأطفال وسائر الأمراض الرهيبة.

■ Restez en bonne santé. Prenez le vaccin oral contre la poliomyélite.
■ «Wellbee» desea lo mejor para su salud. Tome la vacuna antipoliomielítica oral. ■ "Wellbee" – это значит "чувствуйте себя хорошо". Принимайте пероральную вакцину против полиомиелита. ■ "维尔比" 说：要健康，就用口服脊灰疫苗。
■ لتكن في خير صحة وعافية. تناول لقاح شلل الأطفال الفموي.

■ Gain this vaccination diploma. Let's make all Ecuadorian children happy, strong and healthy.
■ Obtenez ce diplôme de vaccination. Il faut que tous les enfants équatoriens soient heureux, forts et en bonne santé. ■ Получи сертификат вакцинации, сделай всех эквадорских детей счастливыми, сильными и здоровыми. ■ 赢得这份计划免疫奖状。为了厄瓜多尔所有儿童的幸福、强壮和健康，让我们一起努力。

■ امنح نفسك هذه الشهادة. لنجعل كل أطفال إكوادور سعداء وأقوياء وأصحاء.

■ Polio: don't paralyse his dreams. ■ Poliomyélite : pour que ses rêves ne soient pas paralysés. ■ Полиомиелит: не дайте ему парализовать вашу мечту. ■ 接种了疫苗，脊灰：不要让它使你的梦想落空。

■ شلل الأطفال: لا تجهزوا على حلمه.

- Remember, a vaccinated child is a protected child.
- Recuerde: un niño vacunado es un niño protegido.
- Помните! Вакцинированный ребенок – это защищенный ребенок.
- 请铭记：孩子接种了疫苗，就得到了保护。
- تذكروا أن حماية الطفل تعني تطعيمه.

- If you have a problem, don't delay. Seek treatment.
- Si vous avez des problèmes, ne tardez pas. Consultez.
- Si tienes un problema, busca tratamiento cuanto antes.
- Если у вас возникла проблема, не откладывайте. Обращайтесь за лечением.
- 遇有身体不适，请不要拖延。要设法求治。
- إذا واجهتك مشكلة صحية اطلب العلاج فوراً.

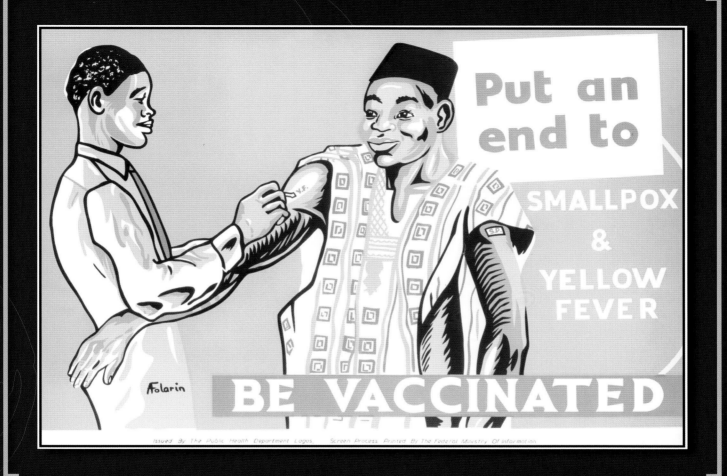

■ Sus à la variole et à la fièvre jaune : faites-vous vacciner ! ■ Ayúdenos a acabar con la viruela y la fiebre amarilla. Vacúnese.
■ Положи конец оспе и желтой лихорадке — вакцинируйся! ■ 祛除天花和黄热病，请接种疫苗。
■ ضعوا حداً للجدري والحمى الصفراء. عليكم بالتطعيم.

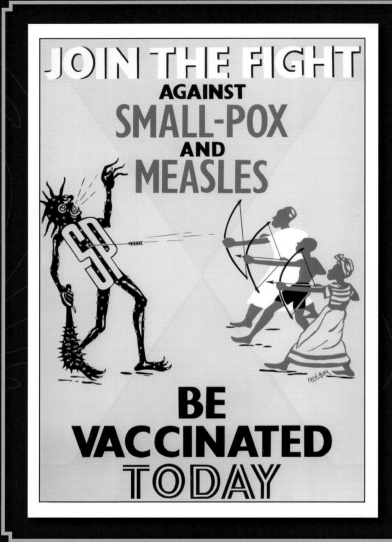

■ Participez à la lutte contre la variole et la rougeole. Faites-vous vacciner aujourd'hui même. ■ Únase a la lucha contra la viruela y el sarampión. Vacúnese hoy mismo. ■ Присоединяйтесь к борьбе против оспы и кори - вакцинируйтесь сегодня же! ■ 加入控制天花和麻疹行列。今天就接种疫苗。

■ انضموا إلى مكافحة الجدري والحصبة. عليكم بالتطعيم اليوم.

■ Evitez la variole. Faites-vous vacciner aujourd'hui même. ■ Protéjase contra la viruela. Vacúnese hoy mismo. ■ Избегаете оспы! Вакцинируйтесь сегодня же! ■ 远离天花。请在今天接种疫苗。

■ تجنبوا الإصابة بالجدري. عليكم بالتطعيم اليوم.

予防为主 **YU FANG WEIZHU**

■ Poster promoting youth vaccination for smallpox and measles. ■ Affiche visant à promouvoir la vaccination contre la variole et la rougeole auprès des jeunes. ■ Cartel en el que ya se promueve la vacunación de la población joven contra la viruela y el sarampión. ■ Плакат, пропагандирующий вакцинацию против оспы и кори. ■ 鼓励年轻人接种天花和麻疹疫苗的海报。

■ لابد من تعزيز تطعيم الشباب من أجل الوقاية من الجدري والحصبة.

13

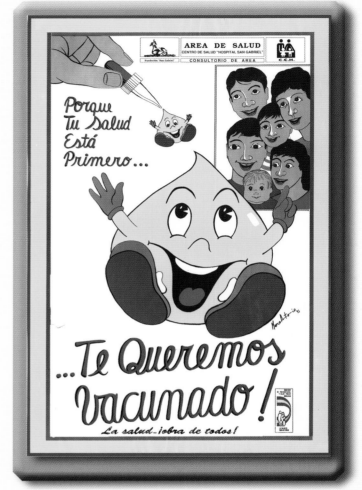

■ Vaccinated children are protected children. The Ministry of Health offers you the new combined measles-mumps-rubella vaccine for free.
■ Un niño vacunado es un niño protegido. El Ministerio de Salud ofrece gratuitamente la nueva vacuna combinada contra el sarampión, la rubéola y las paperas. ■ Вакцинированные дети – защищённые дети. Министерство здравоохранения бесплатно предоставляет вам новую комбинированную вакцину против кори, краснухи, эпидемического паротита. ■ 儿童接种了疫苗，就得到了保护：卫生部免费提供麻疹、流行性腮腺炎和风疹联合疫苗。

■ حماية الأطفال تعني تطعيمهم. وزارة الصحة تعرض مجانا إعطاء اللقاح الجديد ضد الحصبة والحصبة الألمانية والنكاف.

■ Because your health comes first….we want you vaccinated. Health - Everybody's task! ■ Parce que ta santé est prioritaire … nous voulons que tu sois vacciné ! La santé, c'est l'affaire de tous !
■ Твое здоровье является самым важным, поэтому мы хотим, чтобы ты вакцинировался! Здоровье – обязанность всех и каждого! ■ 由于您的健康优先，我们期望您接种疫苗！健康——每个人的任务！！

■ نريد تطعيمك لأن صحتك أهم من أي شيء. الصحة مهمة الجميع!

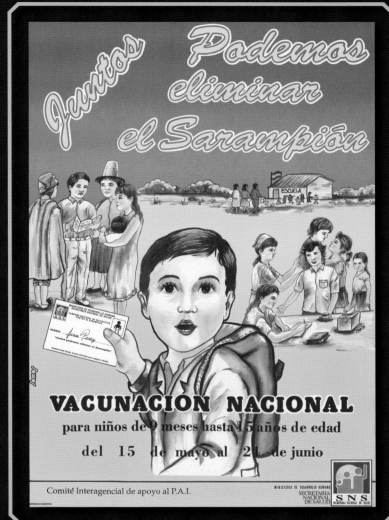

■ Immunizing our children is our duty. ■ Vacciner nos enfants est notre devoir. ■ Inmunizar a nuestros hijos es un deber. ■ Иммунизировать детей – наша обязанность. ■ 为儿童接种疫苗，是我们的责任。

■ Together we can eliminate measles. National vaccination for children from 9 months to 15 years of age. ■ Ensemble, nous pouvons éliminer la rougeole. Vaccination nationale pour les enfants âgés de 9 mois à 15 ans. ■ Вместе мы можем ликвидировать корь. Национальная вакцинация детей в возрасте от 9 месяцев до 15 лет. ■ 只有共同努力，我们才能消灭麻疹。国家疫苗接种，针对9个月龄至15岁的儿童。

■ نستطيع معاً التخلص من الحصبة. الحملة الوطنية لتطعيم الأطفال من سن 9 شهور إلى 15 عاماً.

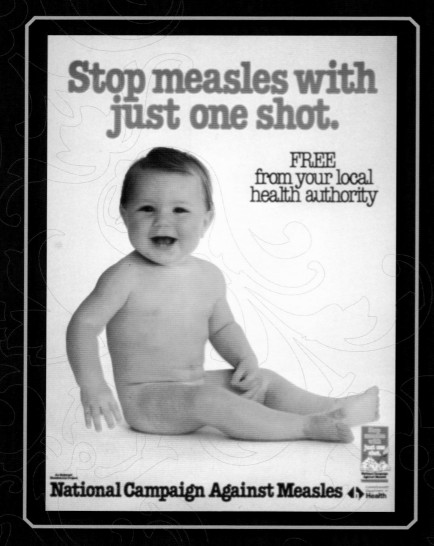

■ Stopper la rougeole au moyen d'une seule piqûre. ■ Pongamos fin al sarampión con una sola inyección. ■ Остановить корь одним уколом. ■ 只需打一针，就能遏制麻疹。

■ لندحر الحصبة بحقنة واحدة.

■ Vaccinated children are healthy: TB, diptheria, tetanus, polio, whooping cough, chicken pox. ■ Les enfants vaccinés sont bien portants : tuberculose, diphtérie, tétanos, poliomyélite, coqueluche, varicelle. ■ Un niño vacunado es un niño sano: tuberculosis, difteria, tétanos, poliomielitis, tos ferina, varicela. ■ Вакцинированные дети – здоровые дети: ТБ, дифтерит, столбняк, полиомиелит, коклюш, ветрянка. ■ 接种疫苗，保儿童健康：结核病、白喉、破伤风、脊灰、百日咳、水痘。

■ الأطفال المطعمون أطفال أصحاء: التطعيم ضد السل والخناق والتيتانوس وشلل الأطفال والشاهوق والجديري.

■ Now is the time for Indonesia to be free of polio. Bring your children in for a free polio vaccination at the PIN service post. ■ Le moment est venu pour l'Indonésie de se libérer de la poliomyélite : amenez vos enfants aux postes des services PIN pour les faire vacciner gratuitement. ■ Ha llegado el momento de que Indonesia acabe con la poliomielitis: acuda con sus hijos al servicio nacional de inmunización para que le administren gratuitamente la vacuna antipoliomielítica. ■ Для Индонезии настало время освободиться от полиомиелита: приведите своих детей в медпункт PIN для бесплатной иммунизации. ■ 现在，印度尼西亚到了无脊灰时刻：把你的孩子带到国家计划免疫运动（PIN）服务站，免费接种脊灰疫苗。

■ آن الأوان لتحرير إندونيسيا من شلل الأطفال: أحضروا أطفالكم إلى المركز الصحي لتطعيمهم ضد شلل الأطفال.

■ They are not equals: vaccination makes the difference. ■ Ils ne sont pas égaux. C'est la vaccination qui fait la différence. ■ No han tenido la misma suerte. La vacunación marca la diferencia. ■ Они неравны. Разница в вакцинации. ■ 他们不一样：免疫接种带来变化。

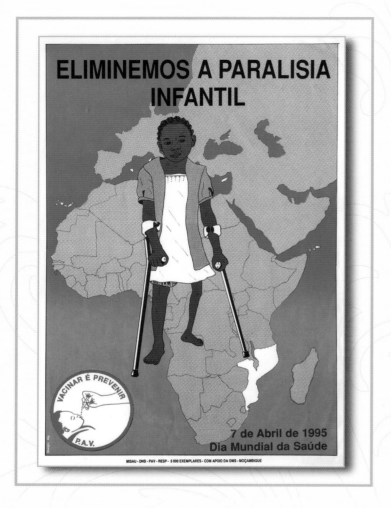

■ Let's eliminate child paralysis. ■ Eliminons la paralysie infantile.
■ Acabemos con la parálisis infantil. ■ Ликвидируем детский
паралич. ■ 让我们消灭儿童麻痹。

■ لنتخلص من شلل الأطفال.

■ Tetanus toxoid vaccination. ■ Vaccination antitétanique. ■ Vacunación
con anatoxina tetánica. ■ Вакцинация столбнячным анатоксином.
■ 接种破伤风类毒素。

■ التطعيم بالذيفان المعطل للتيتانوس.

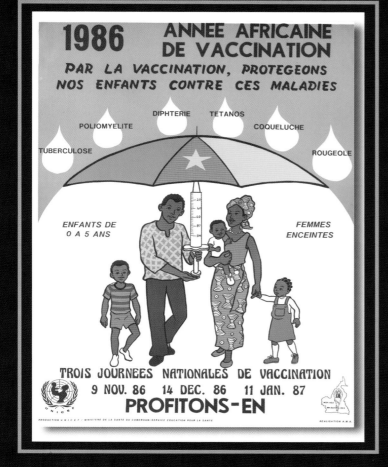

■ 1986: African Vaccination Year. Through vaccination let's protect our children against these diseases: tuberculosis, poliomyelitis, diphtheria, tetanus, whooping cough and measles. ■ 1986: Año Africano de Vacunación. Vacunemos a nuestros niños para protegerlos contra estas enfermedades: tuberculosis, poliomielitis, difteria, tétanos, tos ferina y sarampión. ■ 1986 г. – год вакцинации в Африке: с помощью вакцинации защитим наших детей от таких болезней, как туберкулез, полиомиелит, дифтерия, столбняк, коклюш и корь. Дети от рождения до пяти лет и беременные женщины. Три национальных дня вакцинации. ■ 1986非洲计划免疫年：通过接种疫苗，儿童可防患以下疾病：结核病、脊髓灰质炎、白喉、破伤风、百日咳和麻疹。针对0至5岁儿童和孕妇。

■ عام 1986 هو عام التطعيم في أفريقيا. بفضل التطعيم نحمي أطفالنا من أمراض السل وشلل الأطفال والخناق والتيتانوس والشاهوق والحصبة.

■ Great national mobilization for vaccination on 16 October: polio, whooping cough, measles. For the life of your child … ■ Grande mobilisation nationale pour la vaccination le 16 octobre. Poliomyélite, coqueluche, rougeole. Pour la vie de votre enfant … ■ 16 октября этого года - широкая национальная кампания по мобилизации в целях иммунизации против полиомиелита, коклюша, кори. Для жизни ваших детей… ■ 10月16日，计划免疫全国大动员：脊灰、百日咳、麻疹。为了孩子的生命……

■ حملة الاستنفار الوطني الكبرى من أجل التطعيم في السادس عشر من تشرين الأول/ أكتوبر الحالي: شلل الأطفال والسعال الديكي والحصبة. من أجل حياة أطفالكم…

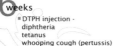

immunisation 2000

Protect YOUR child

FREE immunisation programme

6 weeks
- DTPH injection - diphtheria tetanus whooping cough (pertussis) Hib
- Hepatitis B injection
- Polio sip

3 months
- DTPH injection
- Hepatitis B injection
- Polio sip

5 months
- DTPH injection
- Hepatitis B injection
- Polio sip

15 months
- DTPH injection
- MMR injection - measles mumps rubella

11 years
- MMR injection
- Td injection - tetanus diphtheria
- Polio sip

MINISTRY OF HEALTH

WellChild

New Zealand, June 1998. Code 7006

■ Protégez votre enfant: programme de vaccination gratuite. ■ Proteja a su hijo: programa de inmunización gratuita. ■ Защити своего ребенка Программа бесплатной иммунизации. ■ 保护您的孩子：不用掏钱的免疫规划。

عليكم بحماية أطفالكم. برنامج التمنيع المجاني.

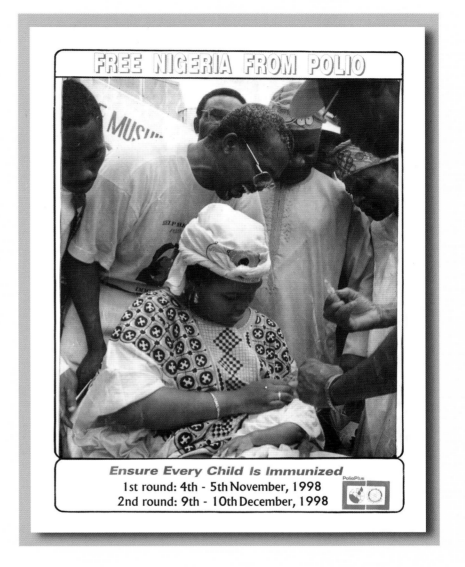

Ensure Every Child Is Immunized
1st round: 4th - 5th November, 1998
2nd round: 9th - 10th December, 1998

■ Protect your child: make sure he gets three doses before his first birthday. ■ Protégez votre enfant en veillant à ce qu'il reçoive les trois doses avant l'âge d'un an. ■ Proteja a su hijo: complete las tres dosis durante el primer año. ■ Защити своего ребенка, завершив иммунизацию тремя дозами в течение первого года жизни.
■ 一岁之内完成三次接种，可为孩子带来保护。

■ Libérez le Nigéria de la poliomyélite. Veillez à ce que chaque enfant soit vacciné. ■ Acabemos con la poliomielitis en Nigeria. Aseguremos la inmunización de todos los niños. ■ Освободим Нигерию от полиомиелита. Обеспечим иммунизацию каждого ребенка. ■ 让尼日利亚摆脱脊灰困扰。确保每位儿童获得免疫。

■ حرروا نيجيريا من شلل الأطفال. أمّنوا التمنيع لكل طفل.

21

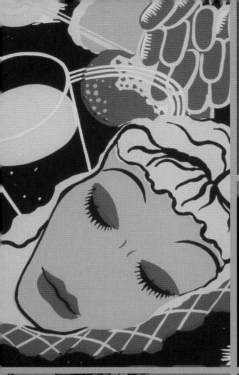

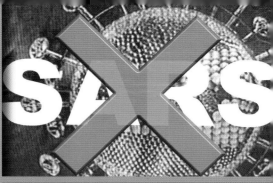

SAXS

预防疾病

Prevenir

Prevent

عليكم بتجنب
الإصابة بالمرض

Prévenir

Prevent. For most of the 19th century, sanitary and environmental reforms were presented as the best ways to defend the public's health against the evils of contagion or dirt-based diseases. The arrival of scientific disciplines like bacteriology, parasitology and virology changed attitudes towards diseases and their control, as microorganisms began to be seen as the primary vehicles spreading life-threatening illness. Infections like tuberculosis and cholera were major killers, so new findings about their impact and how they were passed on were considered very seriously.

All these trends are well presented in the posters showcased in this chapter. Several of them relate to public health campaigns targeting tuberculosis. In the 19th century, the disease was variously thought to be a product of bodily imbalances, imperfect diet, or heredity and genetics. Robert Koch's explanation of the role played by a specific bacterium in causing the disease added to the complexity of explanatory and diagnostic frameworks; a point highlighted by several public health posters which urged cleaner domestic living arrangements, access to exercise and fresh air, personal hygiene and the need to avoid exposure to the tuberculosis bacillus.

The 20th century did witness other public health initiatives, particularly the long-standing battle against malaria which still causes over a million deaths worldwide every year. As the posters show, a variety of tactics were deployed against the disease. The use of protective netting, treatment by quinine and its derivatives, cures through synthetic drugs and the use of chemical pesticides against the mosquitoes capable of transmitting malaria, were important components of eradication programmes in the 1950s and 1960s.

International public health initiatives of this nature have continued especially where there have been major threats from previously unknown diseases, like the outbreak of severe acute respiratory syndrome (SARS) in South-East Asia. Spread by air travellers to Canada, SARS provoked a worldwide alert, travel restrictions and local isolation regimes. The Chinese poster warning about avian flu is a worrying reminder of the potential dangers facing the world today. Along with the well-known public health threats of malaria and tuberculosis, avian flu could yet threaten the well-being of us all.

Prévenir. Pendant la plus grande partie du XIXe siècle, l'amélioration de l'hygiène et de la salubrité de l'environnement était présentée comme le meilleur moyen de défendre la santé publique contre la contagion et les maladies liées à la saleté. L'avènement de disciplines scientifiques comme la bactériologie, la parasitologie et la virologie a modifié les attitudes à l'égard des maladies et de la lutte à mesure qu'on a commencé à considérer les micro-organismes comme les agents responsables en priorité de la propagation de pathologies potentiellement mortelles. Les infections comme la tuberculose et le choléra faisaient un nombre important de victimes et les nouvelles découvertes concernant leur impact et leur propagation ont particulièrement retenu l'attention.

Toutes ces tendances sont apparentes dans les affiches présentées dans ce chapitre. Plusieurs d'entre elles se rapportent à des campagnes de santé publique dirigées contre la tuberculose. Au XIXe siècle, la maladie pouvait apparaître comme le résultat de déséquilibres de l'organisme, d'une mauvaise nutrition ou d'origine héréditaire et génétique. L'explication donnée par Robert Koch du rôle joué par un bacille déterminé a accru la complexité des cadres explicatifs et diagnostiques ; c'est un élément que font ressortir plusieurs affiches de santé publique qui préconisent une meilleure hygiène domestique, l'exercice physique et l'air pur, l'hygiène personnelle et relèvent l'importance d'éviter l'exposition au bacille de la tuberculose.

D'autres initiatives de santé publique ont également marqué le XXe siècle, en particulier la longue lutte contre le paludisme qui, aujourd'hui encore, fait plus d'un million de morts chaque année. Comme le montrent les affiches, différentes tactiques ont été utilisées pour lutter contre la maladie. L'utilisation de moustiquaires de protection, le traitement par la quinine et ses dérivés, le recours à des produits de synthèse et l'utilisation de pesticides chimiques contre le moustique vecteur ont été d'importants aspects des programmes d'éradication du paludisme au cours des années 50 et 60.

Les initiatives internationales de santé publique de ce type se sont poursuivies surtout lorsqu'on a dû faire face à des menaces majeures dues à des maladies précédemment inconnues, comme la flambée du syndrome respiratoire aigu sévère (SRAS) en Asie du Sud-Est. Propagé par avion vers le Canada par des voyageurs infectés, le SRAS a entraîné une alerte mondiale, des restrictions de déplacement et des régimes d'isolement. L'affiche chinoise mettant en garde contre la grippe aviaire nous rappelle les menaces potentielles auxquelles le monde doit faire face. Au même titre que les menaces bien connues que constituent la tuberculose et le paludisme, la grippe aviaire peut menacer notre bien-être à tous.

Prevenir. Durante la mayor parte del siglo XIX las reformas sanitarias y ambientales se presentaron como la mejor opción para defender la salud de la población frente al peligro de las enfermedades contagiables o causadas por la falta de higiene. El nacimiento de disciplinas científicas como la bacteriología, la parasitología y la virología hizo que cambiara la actitud respecto a las enfermedades y a la manera de combatirlas, pues se empezó a considerar que los microorganismos eran los vehículos principales de la transmisión de enfermedades potencialmente mortales. Infecciones como la tuberculosis y el cólera se cobraban gran número de vidas, por lo que los nuevos hallazgos acerca de su impacto y sus modalidades de transmisión fueron tenidos en cuenta muy seriamente.

Todas esas tendencias están bien reflejadas en los carteles mostrados en este capítulo. Varios de ellos se inscriben en campañas de salud pública centradas en la tuberculosis. En el siglo XIX se creía según distintas interpretaciones que la enfermedad se debía a desequilibrios orgánicos, a una mala alimentación o a factores hereditarios o genéticos. Las ideas de Robert Koch sobre la función de una bacteria específica vinieron a acentuar la complejidad de los marcos explicativos y diagnósticos, centrando la atención en un aspecto resaltado por varios carteles de salud pública en que se urgía a mantener limpio el ámbito doméstico, practicar ejercicio y respirar aire puro, cuidar la higiene personal y evitar la exposición al bacilo de la tuberculosis.

El siglo XX fue testigo de otras iniciativas de salud pública, en particular de la larga batalla contra la malaria, que causa aún más de un millón de muertes en todo el mundo cada año. Los carteles reflejan las diversas tácticas desplegadas contra la enfermedad. El uso de mosquiteros de protección, el tratamiento con quinina y sus derivados, los remedios a base de fármacos sintéticos y el uso de plaguicidas contra los mosquitos capaces de transmitir la malaria fueron todos ellos importantes componentes de los programas de erradicación de la enfermedad en los años cincuenta y sesenta.

Han seguido luego otras iniciativas internacionales de salud pública similares, sobre todo ante amenazas importantes planteadas por enfermedades antes desconocidas, como el brote de síndrome respiratorio agudo severo (SRAS) en Asia sudoriental. Propagado por los pasajeros de un vuelo al Canadá, el SRAS provocó una alerta mundial, restricciones de los viajes y medidas de aislamiento locales. El cartel donde se advierte en chino sobre la gripe aviar es un preocupante recordatorio de los peligros potenciales que afronta el mundo. Junto con las bien conocidas amenazas para la salud pública que suponen la malaria y la tuberculosis, la gripe aviar podría volver a perturbar el bienestar de todos nosotros.

Избегайте опасности. В течение большей части 19-го столетия изменения санитарии и экологии представлялись как наилучшие способы защитить здоровье населения от опасностей заражения или болезней, связанных с плохой гигиеной. Появление таких научных дисциплин, как бактериология, паразитология и вирусология, изменили позиции по отношению к болезням и борьбе с ними, так как микроорганизмы стали рассматриваться как основные средства распространения болезней, угрожающих жизни. Такие инфекции, как туберкулез и холера, были главными убийцами, и новые открытия об их воздействии и передаче воспринимались очень серьезно.

Все эти тенденции достаточно хорошо отражены в плакатах, показанных в этой главе. Некоторые из них связаны с кампаниями общественного здравоохранения, ориентированными на туберкулез. В 19-ом столетии эта болезнь различным образом считалась результатом отсутствия баланса в организме, неправильного рациона питания, или же как наследственная и генетическая. Объяснение Роберта Коха роли, которую играют конкретные бактерии в возникновений болезни, еще более усложнило пояснительные и диагностические рамки; и именно это было подчеркнуто в ряде плакатов общественного здравоохранения, которые призывали к более чистым условиям жизни в быту, доступу к физическим упражнениям и свежему воздуху, личной гигиене и к необходимости избегать воздействия туберкулезных бацилл.

В 20-ом столетии были предприняты другие инициативы общественного здравоохранения, особенно - длительная борьба против малярии, которая продолжает вызывать миллионы случаев смерти во всем мире ежегодно. Как показывают плакаты, против этой болезни предпринималась разнообразная тактика. Использование защитных сеток, лечение хинином и его дериватами, лечение с помощью синтетических лекарств и использование химических пестицидов против комаров, способных передавать малярию, были важными компонентами программ ликвидации малярии в 1950-е и 1960-е годы.

Международные инициативы общественного здравоохранения такого характера продолжались особенно в тех случаях, когда существовала серьезная угроза от болезней, которые ранее не были известны, такие как вспышка тяжелого острого респираторного синдрома (ТОРС) в Юго-Восточной Азии. Распространившись через авиапассажиров в Канаду, она вызвала обеспокоенность во всем мире, привела к ограничениям на поездки и режимам местной изоляции. Китайский плакат, предупреждающий о птичьем гриппе, является серьезным напоминанием о потенциальных опасностях, с которыми мир сталкивается сегодня. Наряду с хорошо известными угрозами для общественного здравоохранения со стороны малярии и туберкулеза, птичий грипп может угрожать благополучию всех нас.

预防疾病。 在19世纪的大多时间内，卫生和环境变革被看作保护公众健康，防患传染病或不卫生疾病的最佳方式。细菌学、寄生虫病学和病毒学等科学学科的问世，改变了人们对疾病及其控制的看法。微生物开始被看作传播致命疾病的首要载体。结核病和霍乱等感染成为主要杀手，因此，在传染病带来的影响及其传播方式方面的新发现得到了高度重视。

本章节中描述的海报很好地介绍了这些发展趋势。其中一些海报是以结核病为目标的公共卫生宣传活动。在19世纪，疾病又被认为属于身体失衡、饮食不良或遗传和基因的产物等不同情况。罗伯特·科赫解释了特定致病细菌所发挥的作用，这更增加了说明和诊断框架的复杂性。几个公共卫生海报都强调了这一点，这些海报要求创造更加清洁的居家环境、能够锻炼并保持空气清新、讲究个人卫生并要避免接触结核杆菌。

20世纪确实见证了其它一些公共卫生行动，特别是长期以来向疟疾发出的攻击，至今该病在世界上每年仍造成100多万人死亡。正如海报所展示的，曾经采取了不同的办法来控制这个疾病。在50和60年代，消除规划采用的主要方法有：使用保护性蚊帐；用奎宁及其衍生物进行治疗；使用合成药物治疗；使用化学杀虫剂，杀死可传播疟疾的蚊子。

这类国际公共卫生行动一直延续下来，特别是当遇到类似在东南亚发生的严重急性呼吸道综合征（SARS，又称传染性非典型肺炎）等不明原因疾病带来的重大威胁时。SARS通过飞机乘客传到了加拿大，它引起了全世界的警觉，导致发布了旅行限制，并促成了地方隔离管理制度。中国警告禽流感的海报就是当今世界面临禽流感潜在威胁的提示，这令人十分担心。如果再加上疟疾和结核病已知对公共卫生带来的威胁，禽流感可危及我们所有人的安康。

عليكم بتجنب الإصابة بالمرض. خلال القسط الأعظم من القرن التاسع عشر قُدمت عمليات الإصلاح الإصحاحي والبيئي على أنها أفضل الطرق لحماية الصحة من شرور الأمراض المعدية أو الأمراض التي مصدرها الأقذار. وقد أدى نشوء تخصصات علمية من قبيل علم الجراثيم وعلم الطفيليات وعلم الفيروسات إلى تغيير النظرة إلى الأمراض ومكافحتها، وبدأ يُنظر إلى الكائنات المجهرية على أنها النواقل الرئيسية التي تنشر الاعتلالات التي تهدد الحياة. وكانت الأمراض المعدية، مثل السل والكوليرا، هي أهم الأمراض القاتلة، لذا فقد تم التركيز بجدية شديدة على الاستنتاجات الجديدة الخاصة بأثرها وطرق انتقالها.

وقد نزعت هذه النزعات إلى حد بعيد على الملصقات الإعلانية المعروضة في هذا الفصل. وخلال القرن التاسع عشر كان يُظن، بطرق مختلفة أن المرض ينتج عن اختلالات في توازن الجسم وعيوب النظام الغذائي أو الوراثة والوراثيات. وكان تفسير روبرت كوخ للدور الذي تلعبه جرثومة معينة من الأمور التي زادت من تعقيد الأطر التفسيرية والتشخيصية. وكانت تلك من النقاط التي أبرزتها ملصقات إعلانية عديدة خاصة بالصحة العمومية حضت على اتخاذ ترتيبات أنظف للمعيشة في المنزل، وعلى ممارسة التمارين الرياضية وعلى الهواء النقي وعادات النظافة الشخصية وضرورة تجنب التعرض لجرثومة السل العصوية.

وقد شهد القرن العشرون بالفعل مبادرات أخرى في مجال الصحة العمومية، وخصوصاً المعركة القديمة ضد الملاريا، وهي المرض الذي مازال يتسبب في أكثر من مليون وفاة في العالم سنوياً. ومثلما تظهره الملصقات الإعلانية فقد استُخدمت مجموعة متنوعة من الأساليب في مكافحة هذا المرض. وكان من أهم عناصر برامج استئصال الملاريا في الخمسينات والستينات من القرن العشرين استخدام الناموسيات الواقية والعلاج بدواء كينين ومشتقاته والعلاجات التي استُخدمت فيها أدوية تخليقية واستخدام مبيدات الهوام الكيميائية المضادة للبعوض القادر على نقل الملاريا.

واستمرت المبادرات الدولية ذات الطابع المماثل في مجال الصحة العمومية، وخصوصاً حيثما وجدت أخطار كبرى نتيجة أمراض لم تكن معروفة في السابق، مثل تفشي المتلازمة التنفسية الحادة الوخيمة (سارس) في جنوب شرق آسيا. وقد أدت هذه المتلازمة، التي انتشرت عن طريق المسافرين جواً إلى كندا، إلى إطلاق إنذار عالمي وتسببت في فرض قيود على السفر وفي فرض نُظم عزل محلية. كما أن الملصق الإعلاني الصيني الذي يحذر من أنفلونزا الطيور هو تذكرة تحذيرية بالأخطار المحتملة التي يواجهها العالم اليوم، وعلاوة على التهديدات المعروفة جيداً في مجال الصحة العمومية جراء الملاريا والسل، فان أنفلونزا الطيور ما زالت تشكل تهديداً لعافيتنا جميعاً.

■ "Veterans" National Tuberculosis Patients' Day. ■ Día Nacional de los Enfermos Tuberculosos, dedicado a los «Veteranos de Guerra». ■ Национальный день помощи больным туберкулезом, посвященный ветеранам. ■ "老兵" 全国结核病患者日。

■ «المحاربون القدامى». اليوم الوطني لمرضى السل.

■ "Veterans: Let's save them." National Tuberculosis Patients' Day.
■ «Salvemos a los veteranos de guerra». Día Nacional de los Enfermos Tuberculosos. ■ "Спасем ветеранов." Национальный день помощи больным туберкулезом. ■ "老兵：让我们来拯救" 全国结核病患者日。

■ علينا بإنقاذ «المحاربين القدامى». اليوم الوطني لمرضى السل.

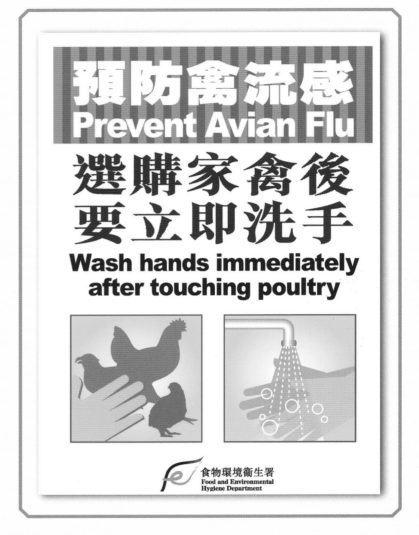

■ Let's unite to fight SARS. ■ Unissons-nous pour lutter contre le SRAS. ■ Unamos nuestras fuerzas para combatir el SRAS. ■ Объединимся в борьбе против ТОРС.

■ وحدوا جهودكم من أجل مكافحة المتلازمة التنفسية الحادة الوخيمة (سارس).

■ Prévenir la grippe aviaire. Se laver immédiatement les mains après avoir touché une volaille. ■ Prevención de la gripe aviar. Si toca un ave de corral, lávese las manos de inmediato. ■ Профилактика птичьего гриппа. Мойте руки сразу же после контакта с птицей.

■ الوقاية من أنفلونزا الطيور. اغسل يديك فوراً بعد ملامسة الدواجن.

■ Let's take action to prevent and treat SARS. ■ Employons-nous activement à prévenir et traiter le SRAS. ■ Adoptemos medidas activas para prevenir y tratar el SRAS. ■ Будем активно проводить профилактику и лечение ТОРС .

■ انشطوا في توقي وعلاج المتلازمة التنفسية الحادة الوخيمة (سارس).

■ To control malaria in your house, spray pesticides and cooperate with the people who come to spray your house. ■ Pour combattre le paludisme chez vous, utilisez des insecticides et facilitez le travail des agents de pulvérisation. ■ Para evitar la malaria en tu hogar, rocía el espacio con plaguicidas y coopera con quienes te visiten para rociar la vivienda. ■ Для борьбы с малярией в вашем доме распыляйте пестициды и сотрудничайте с людьми, которые приходят в ваш дом для распыления пестицидов. ■ 要在家里防范疟疾，就要喷洒杀虫剂并与来到你家喷洒药物的人员配合。

■ لمكافحة الملاريا في منازلكم عليكم برش مبيدات الآفات وبالتعاون مع من يأتون لرش منازلكم.

■ Restez en forme … faites votre test maintenant.
■ Manténgase en forma … acuda ya a su médico para una revisión. ■ Будь в форме … пройди тест сейчас. ■ 保持健康……现在就去检查身体。

■ حافظ على لياقتك ... أجر الاختبار الآن.

1. От чахотки (туберкулеза) ежегодно умирают сотни тысяч людей. Грязное, сырое и темное жилище—рассадник туберкулеза.

Издательство Наркомздрава

■ Hundreds of thousands of people die from TB every year. Dirty, damp and dark homes are breeding grounds for TB. ■ La tuberculose fait des centaines de milliers de morts chaque année. Le bacille de la tuberculose affectionne les habitations sales, humides et sombres. ■ La tuberculosis se cobra cada año la vida de cientos de miles de personas. Las viviendas sucias, húmedas y oscuras son el caldo de cultivo perfecto para esta enfermedad. ■ 每年有成千上万的人死于结核病。家里肮脏、潮湿且昏暗，是结核病的温床。

■ مئات الآلاف يموتون من جراء الإصابة بالسل سنوياً. المنازل القذرة والرطبة والمظلمة بيئة يترعرع فيها السل.

2. Зараза чахотки (туберкулеза) содержится в мокроте больных. Не плюйте на пол.

Издательство Наркомздрава

■ TB infection is present in infected people's phlegm. Don't spit on the floor! ■ Le bacille de la tuberculose est présent dans les crachats des sujets infectés. Ne crachez pas par terre! ■ El bacilo de la tuberculosis se esconde en el esputo. ¡No escupa en el piso! ■ 结核病人的痰中存有感染菌。请不要随地吐痰！

■ عدوى السل موجودة في بلغم المصابين بعدواه. لا تبصقوا على الأرض.

6. Зараза чахотки (туберкулеза) передается через посуду. Мойте посуду горячей водой. Не ешьте из общей чашки.

Т. 20000. Моссублит № 16386. Издательство Наркомздрава. Типо-лит. им. т. Дунаева, Москва, Б. Полянка 9.

4. Чистое, светлое жилище—защита от чахотки (туберкулеза). Дайте доступ в ваше жилище солнечному свету и свежему воздуху.

Издательство Наркомздрава. Т. 30000. Моссублит № 16388. Типо-лит. им. т. Дунаева, Москва, Б. Полянка 9.

■ A light and clean home guards against TB. Let sunlight and fresh air into your home. ■ Un logement propre et bien éclairé est mieux protégé contre la tuberculose. Laissez entrer le soleil et aérez votre logement. ■ Una vivienda limpia y luminosa es una buena protección contra la tuberculosis. Deje que los rayos del sol y el aire fresco inunden su hogar. ■ 家里保持明亮洁净，可防范结核病。让阳光和新鲜空气入室。

■ المنزل النظيف الذي يملؤه النور يحميكم من السل. دعوا ضوء الشمس والهواء النقي يدخلان منازلكم.

■ TB infection can be transmitted by crockery. Wash plates in hot water and don't eat from the same plate. ■ Le bacille de la tuberculose peut se transmettre par la vaisselle. Lavez la vaisselle à l'eau chaude et ne mangez pas tous dans la même assiette. ■ La tuberculosis puede transmitirse a través de la vajilla. Utilice agua caliente para fregar y no coma del mismo plato que otras personas. ■ 陶器可传播结核病。请用热水洗盘子，不要使用同一个盘子用餐。

■ الأواني الفخارية يمكن أن تنقل عدوى السل. اغسلوا الأطباق بالماء الساخن ولا تأكلوا في طبق واحد معاً.

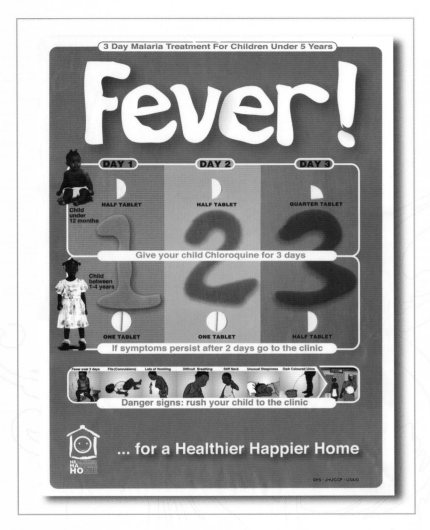

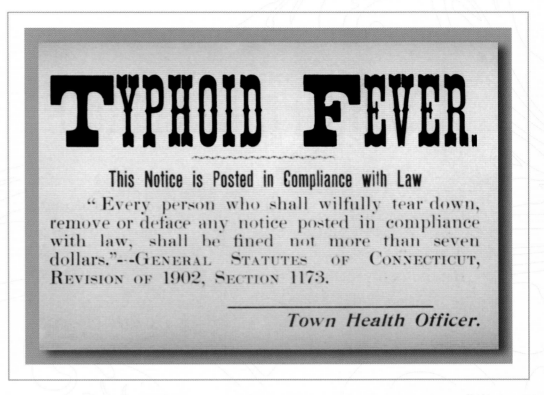

■ Fièvre typhoïde. ■ Fiebre tifoidea. ■ Брюшной тиф. ■ 伤寒。
■ الحمى التيفية.

■ Contre la fièvre: traitement antipaludique de 3 jours destiné aux enfants de moins de 5 ans – Donnez à votre enfant de la chloroquine pendant 3 jours: si les symptômes persistent après 2 jours, allez au dispensaire. En cas de signes de danger, emmenez votre enfant rapidement au dispensaire. Pour une vie familiale plus saine et plus heureuse. ■ ¡Fiebre! Tratamiento antipalúdico de tres días para los menores de 5 años. Déle a su hijo cloroquina durante tres días. Si los síntomas no remiten al cabo del segundo día, acuda a su centro médico. Ante cualquier signo de peligro, lleve a su hijo inmediatamente al hospital. Por un hogar más saludable y feliz. ■ Лихорадка! Трехдневное лечение малярии у детей в возрасте до пяти лет. Давайте вашему ребенку хлорохин в течение 3 дней. Если симптомы продолжатся после двух дней, обратитесь в больницу. Если есть признаки опасности, быстро обратитесь в больницу: … чтобы ваш дом был здоровым и счастливым. ■ 发热！五岁以下儿童的3天疟疾治疗方案：让孩子服用氯喹，连服3天。如两天后症状未变，到诊所就医。出现危险体征时：将孩子快速送往诊所。为的是，有一个更健康、更幸福的家。

■ الحمى: علاج الأطفال دون سن الخامسة لمدة 3 أيام: أعطوا أطفالكم دواء كلوروكين لمدة 3 أيام: إذا استمرت الأعراض بعد يومين اذهبوا إلى العيادة: إذا ظهرت العلامات الخطيرة: أحضروا أطفالكم بسرعة إلى العيادة: ... من أجل منزل مفعم بصحة وسعادة أكثر.

■ Protégez votre enfant du paludisme. Veillez à ce qu'il dorme chaque nuit sous une moustiquaire imprégnée. ■ Proteja a su hijo contra la malaria. Asegúrese de que duerma todas las noches bajo un mosquitero debidamente tratado. ■ Защитите своего ребенка от малярии. Обеспечьте, чтобы ваш ребенок каждую ночь спал под обработанной противомоскитной сеткой. ■ 保护孩子不患疟疾：确保您的孩子，每晚在经过药物处理的蚊帐内睡觉。

■ احموا أطفالكم من الملاريا: احرصوا على أن ينام أطفالكم تحت ناموسية معالجة كل ليلة.

■ Have you been coughing for more than 4 weeks? Go to the health centre: it may be tuberculosis. ■ Toussez-vous depuis plus de 4 semaines ? Allez vite au centre de santé, c'est peut-être la tuberculose. ■ ¿Lleva usted tosiendo más de 4 semanas? Acuda a su centro de salud: podría ser tuberculosis. ■ У тебя кашель больше 4 недель? Обратись в медпункт – это может быть туберкулез. ■ 咳嗽已经超过4周了吗？到医院检查一下，可能得了结核病。

■ هل تعاني من السعال منذ أكثر من 4 أسابيع؟ اذهب إلى المركز الصحي فقد تكون مصابا بالسل.

■ Utilisez davantage la stratégie DOTS. C'est le bon moyen de guérir la tuberculose.
■ Extendamos la utilización del DOTS. El tratamiento DOTS: una solución óptima para curar la tuberculosis. ■ Шире используйте стратегию ДОТС. Этот курс - правильное направление для излечения от туберкулеза. ■ 扩大使用DOTS！这是治愈结核病的好办法。

■ استعملوا المعالجة القصيرة الأمد للسل تحت الإشراف المباشر (DOTS) على نطاق أوسع! إنها تضعكم على المسار السليم للشفاء من السل.

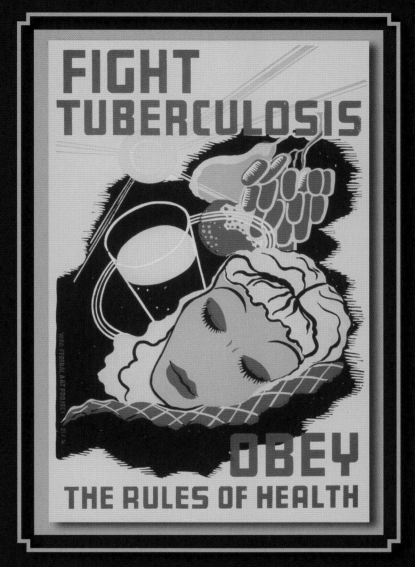

■ Lutte contre la tuberculose – Respectez les règles de la santé.
■ Combatamos la tuberculosis. Respete las normas de salud.
■ Борись с туберкулезом – подчиняйся правилам охраны здоровья.
■ 抗击结核病——遵守健康规则。

■ كافحوا السل - أطيعوا قواعد الصحة.

By striving for healthy living conditions we'll vanquish TB. ■ Des conditions de vie saines nous permettront de vaincre la tuberculose. ■ Nuestros esfuerzos por lograr modos de vida saludables nos ayudarán a eliminar la tuberculosis. ■ 营造健康的生活环境，让结核病销声匿迹。

■ نستطيع دحر السل بكفاحنا من أجل تهيئة الظروف الصحية.

Eliminate mosquitoes on the farm. ■ Eliminer les moustiques à la ferme. ■ Elimine los mosquitos en la granja. ■ 除掉农场的蚊虫。

■ اقضوا على الناموس في المزرعة.

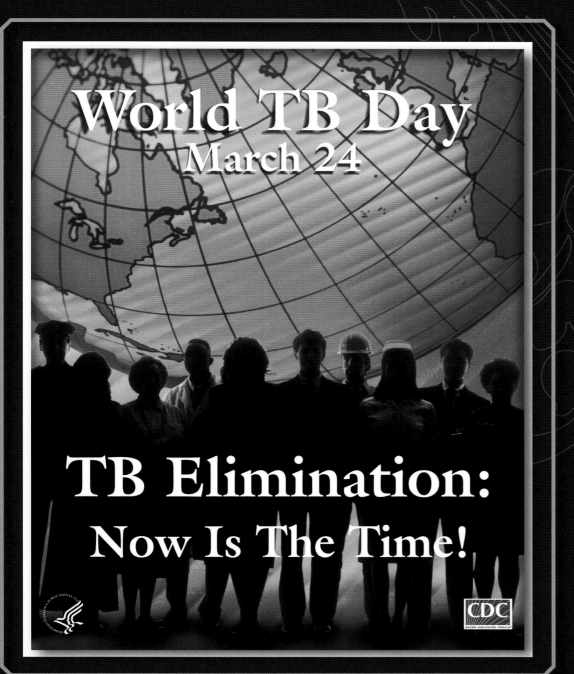

THE NEXT TO GO

FIGHT TUBERCULOSIS!
Red Cross Christmas Seal Campaign

HEALTH Christmas 1924

Buy Christmas Seals

Fight Tuberculosis

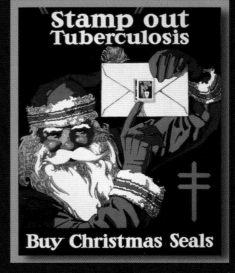

Stamp out Tuberculosis

Buy Christmas Seals

■ Achetez des timbres de Noël . Luttez contre la tuberculose. ■ Compre sellos de Navidad. Combatamos la tuberculosis. ■ Приобретайте новогодние штемпеля. Боритесь с туберкулезом. ■ 购买圣诞封缄：抗击结核病。

■ اشتروا دمغات عيد الميلاد المجيد: كافحوا السل.

■ Supprimons la tuberculose. Achetons des timbres de Noël. ■ Acabemos con la tuberculosis. Compre sellos de Navidad. ■ Уничтожьте туберкулез. Приобретайте новогодние штемпеля. ■ 祛除结核病。购买圣诞封缄。

■ ادحروا السل. اشتروا طوابع عيد الميلاد المجيد.

■ La prochaine victime … Luttons contre la tuberculose. ■ La siguiente víctima... Combatamos la tuberculosis. ■ Ты можешь стать следующей жертвой. Борись с туберкулезом. ■ 下一位罹病者……抗击结核病。

■ الضحية القادمة … فلنكافح السل.

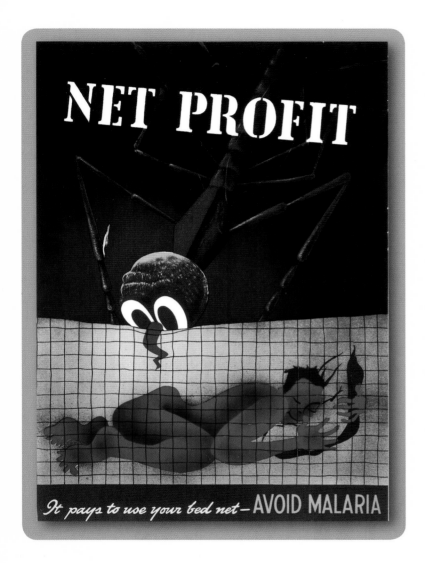

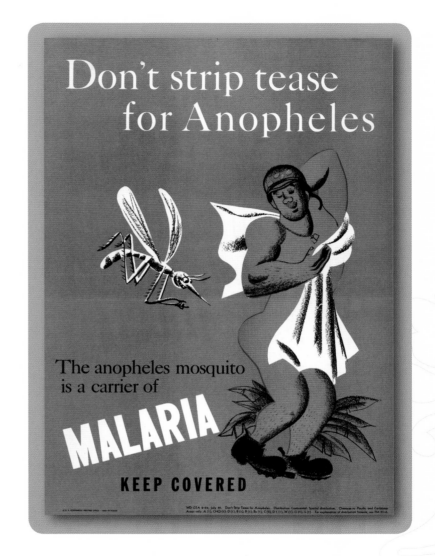

■ Tout bénéfice. Utilisez votre moustiquaire. Evitez le paludisme.
■ Toda una red de beneficios. Siempre merece la pena utilizar el mosquitero. Protéjase contra la malaria. ■ Только выгоды. Использование надкроватной сетки окупается. Избегай малярию.
■ 纯收益。使用蚊帐，你会得益——防患疟疾。

الربح الصافي. من المجدي استعمال الناموسية. تجنبوا الإصابة ■
بالملاريا.

■ On se couvre devant les anophèles. L'anophèle transmet le paludisme. Restez couvert. ■ No se desnude ante Anofeles. El mosquito anofeles es uno de los principales portadores de la malaria. Mantenga el cuerpo bien cubierto. ■ Не раздевайся для кровососущих. Кровососущие комары являются переносчиками малярии. Защити свое тело.
■ 不要裸露身体，惹按蚊叮咬。按蚊携带疟疾。穿好衣服，不裸露。

لا تترك جسمك عارياً وعرضة لبعوض الأنوفيلة. عليك بتغطية جسمك دائماً. ■

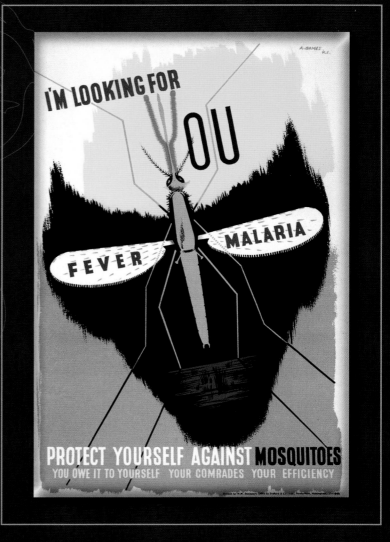

■ Use the new HJ Polzer DDT spray. ■ Utilisons le nouveau pulvérisateur de DDT de HJ Polzer. ■ Utilice el nuevo nebulizador de DDT HJ Polzer. ■ Пользуйтесь новым средством ДДТ спреем "H.J. Polzer". ■ 请使用 DDT新型HJ Polzer自动喷雾剂。

■ لنستعمل بخاخة الـ د د ت الجديدة من صنع شركة هـ جـ بولزر

■ Protégez-vous contre les moustiques. ■ Protéjase contra los mosquitos. ■ Защищайся от комаров. ■ 请您防范蚊子。

■ عليك بحماية نفسك من الناموس.

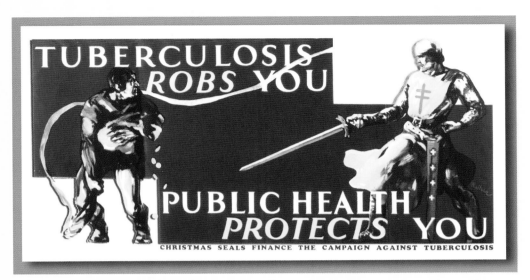

■ La tuberculose vous vole, la santé publique vous protège. ■ La tuberculosis nos estafa. La salud pública nos protege. ■ Туберкулез убивает тебя. Здравоохранение тебя защищает. ■ 结核病掠取你的财物，公共卫生保护你的健康。

■ السل يسلبك ما لديك والصحة العمومية تحميك.

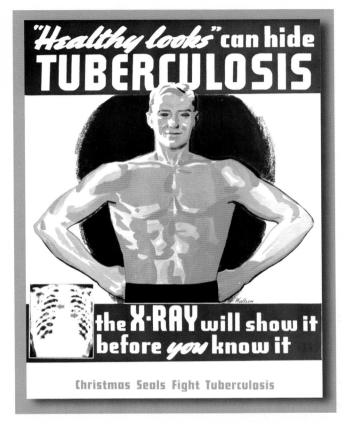

■ Même une bonne mine peut cacher la tuberculose. ■ Detrás de un aspecto saludable puede acechar la tuberculosis. ■ За здоровым видом может скрываться туберкулез. ■ 健康的外表可以掩盖结核病。

■ الشخص الذي يبدو موفور الصحة قد يكون مصاباً بالسل هو الآخر.

■ Luttez contre la tuberculose avec des armes modernes. ■ Combatamos la tuberculosis con armas modernas. ■ Боритесь с туберкулезом современным оружием. ■ 使用现代手段，抗击结核病。

■ حاربوا السل بأسلحة حديثة.

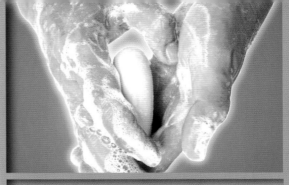

Keep clean

Mantenerse
limpio

Rester propre

保持清洁

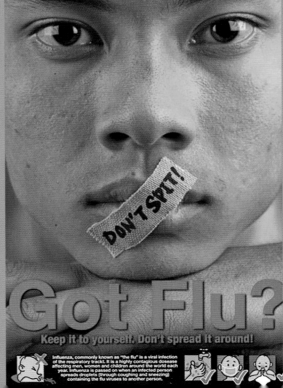

حافظوا على
نظافتكم

Обеспечьте
чистоту

Got Flu?

Keep it to yourself. Don't spread it around!

Influenza, commonly known as "the flu" is a viral infection
of the respiratory tract. It is a highly contagious disease
affecting men, women and children around the world each
year. Influenza is passed on when an infected person
spreads droplets (through coughing and sneezing)
containing the flu viruses to another person.

Keep clean. Hygiene – the set of almost instinctual behaviours that lead us to avoid dirty, disgusting, threatening stuff – is our second immune system. Hygienic behaviour is also good manners. Personal hygiene and environmental cleanliness are exhorted, prized and rewarded by parents, teachers and leaders, and any lapses can have serious consequences for our friendships, our careers – our very status in society.

Every society in the world sets high store by cleanliness. However, occasionally governments decide to demand higher hygiene standards from their populations. Sometimes the reason is a perceived disease threat, sometimes it is an external threat such as war and sometimes the threat is to national identity. Concerns about tuberculosis and influenza in 1920s Europe gave us the memorable slogan, "coughs and sneezes spread diseases". Second World War artists – such as Abram Games in the United Kingdom of Great Britain and Northern Ireland – produced posters illustrating the "dangers of dirt" and warning soldiers about personal cleanliness: "You owe it to your comrades". Post-war nation building saw the promotion of civilized values such as the household toilet, while at the same time the economic progress in richer countries brought soap to every household.

The 1950s saw the first of a series of patriotic hygiene campaigns in China. Observing hygiene rules was a duty that literally served to ferret out pests, diseases and counter-revolutionaries in order to build a new China.

Despite the work of a century, hygiene still remains a problem. It has been calculated that the simple act of washing hands with soap could save over a million lives a year. Promoting hygiene could be one of the most cost-effective means of reaching many health-related development goals. What can these images teach us about how best to go about it? The posters that catch the eye are the attractive ones: the aristocrat with his hanky, the pretty children cleaning their toys, the crocodile with the bird. The images that we remember best are often the ones with simple slogans, whether "keep poop out of the pool" or "a handkerchief in time saves nine". The early posters designed by single artists stand out when compared with the cluttered, over-complicated recent images that show all the hallmarks of design by committee. But which of these images had the most influence on hygiene? The truth is that we simply don't know - finding out how best to change behaviour through visual imagery remains a task to be accomplished in the 21st century.

Rester propre. L'hygiène – une série de comportements presque instinctifs qui nous amènent à éviter tout ce qui est sale, dégoutant ou menaçant – est en quelque sorte notre deuxième système immunitaire. Un comportement respectueux de l'hygiène l'est aussi des bonnes manières. L'hygiène personnelle et la salubrité de l'environnement sont préconisées et récompensées par les parents, par les enseignants et par les dirigeants, et toute carence peut avoir des conséquences graves pour nos amitiés, nos carrières et même notre condition sociale.

La propreté représente quelque chose de primordial pour toutes les sociétés. Il arrive cependant que les pouvoirs publics cherchent à améliorer les normes d'hygiène dans la population, suite à la perception d'une menace de maladie ou d'une menace extérieure comme un conflit ou d'une menace pour l'identité nationale. Les préoccupations liées à la tuberculose et à la grippe dans les années 20 en Europe sont à l'origine de l'idée, érigée en slogan, selon laquelle le fait de tousser et d'éternuer propageait les maladies. Au cours de la seconde guerre mondiale, des artistes comme Abram Games au Royaume-Uni ont créé des affiches illustrant les risques liés à la santé et soulignant l'importance de la propreté personnelle à l'intention des soldats : « Tu le dois à tes camarades » pouvait-on lire. La construction de la nation après la guerre a permis de promouvoir des valeurs civilisatrices comme les W.-C. pour chaque logement alors que les progrès économiques dans les pays plus riches permettaient à chaque famille de disposer de savon.

C'est au cours des années 50 que s'est déroulée la première d'une série de campagnes patriotiques d'hygiène en Chine. Le respect des règles d'hygiène devenait une obligation et il s'agissait d'extirper tous les nuisibles, toutes les infections au même titre que les contre-révolutionnaires, afin d'ériger une Chine nouvelle.

Malgré un bon siècle d'efforts, l'hygiène pose toujours un problème. On a calculé que le simple fait de se laver les mains sauvait plus d'un million de vies par an. La promotion de l'hygiène pourrait être un des moyens les plus rentables d'atteindre une grande partie des objectifs du développement liés à la santé. Comment ces affiches nous renseignent-elles sur les meilleurs moyens d'y parvenir ? Les plus accrocheuses sont celles de l'aristocrate avec son mouchoir, des enfants mignons qui nettoient leurs jouets, du crocodile qui se fait curer les dents par l'oiseau. Celles dont on se souvient le mieux sont souvent celles qui véhiculent des slogans très simples. Les affiches plus anciennes conçues par un seul artiste tranchent nettement avec les travaux plus récents surchargés et peu clairs qui semblent être le fruit de savants compromis obtenus dans le cadre d'un comité. Mais quant à savoir lesquelles de ces illustrations influencent le plus l'hygiène, on a bien du mal à le dire ; découvrir le meilleur moyen de modifier le comportement par l'image reste un défi pour le XXIe siècle.

Mantenerse limpio. La higiene es nuestro segundo sistema inmunitario, algo así como un comportamiento casi instintivo que nos lleva a evitar productos sucios, repugnantes o peligrosos. Una parte del comportamiento higiénico son también las buenas maneras. Los padres, maestros y líderes preconizan, valoran y recompensan la higiene personal y la limpieza del entorno, y cualquier relajación en ese sentido puede repercutir seriamente en nuestras amistades, nuestra profesión o incluso nuestro estatus en la sociedad.

Todas las sociedades del mundo valoran mucho la limpieza. Sin embargo, ocasionalmente los gobiernos se ven obligados a pedir a la población que extremen las medidas de higiene. A veces la razón es la amenaza de una enfermedad, otras veces es una amenaza externa de tipo bélico, y en ocasiones la amenaza afecta a la identidad nacional. La preocupación suscitada por la tuberculosis y la gripe en la Europa de los años veinte se plasmó en un lema memorable: "La tos y los estornudos pueden propagar enfermedades". Artistas que vivieron la Segunda Guerra Mundial, como Abram Games en el Reino Unido de Gran Bretaña e Irlanda del Norte, diseñaron carteles que ilustraban los "peligros de la suciedad" y advertían a los soldados que debían cuidar la higiene personal: "Hazlo por tus camaradas". En el esfuerzo de construcción nacional de posguerra se promovieron avances de sociedades civilizadas como el inodoro en las viviendas, mientras el progreso económico de los países ricos introducía el jabón en todos los hogares.

En los años cincuenta se llevó a cabo la primera de una serie de campañas patrióticas en China. Observar las normas de higiene era un deber que permitió literalmente descubrir plagas, enfermedades y contrarrevolucionarios para construir una nueva China.

Pese a todo lo logrado a lo largo de un siglo, la falta de higiene sigue causando problemas. Se ha calculado que la simple precaución de lavarse las manos con jabón puede salvar la vida a más de un millón de personas cada año. Fomentar la higiene puede ser una de las medidas más costoeficaces para alcanzar muchos objetivos de desarrollo relacionados con la salud. ¿Qué nos enseñan todas esas imágenes sobre la mejor manera de abordar el problema? Los carteles que captan la atención son los más atractivos, como el aristócrata con su pañuelo, esos preciosos niños limpiando sus juguetes, o el cocodrilo y el pájaro. Las imágenes que mejor recordamos suelen ser las que contienen eslóganes muy simples. Los carteles de antaño, diseñados por un solo artista, son claramente reconocibles cuando los comparamos con las imágenes recientes, más densas y sofisticadas, que tienen el sello distintivo del diseño colectivo. Pero ¿cuáles de esas imágenes han tenido más influencia en los hábitos higiénicos? La verdad es que, sencillamente, no lo sabemos: determinar la mejor manera de cambiar los comportamientos mediante estímulos visuales es una tarea pendiente que habrá que acometer en el siglo XXI.

Обеспечьте чистоту. Гигиена является нашей второй иммунной системой; она является набором почти инстинктивных видов поведения, которые ведут нас к тому, чтобы избегать грязных, неприятных, опасных веществ. Гигиенические привычки - это также хорошие манеры. К личной гигиене и чистоте окружающей среды призывают также и вознаграждают за нее родителей, преподавателей и руководителей, и любые оплошности могут иметь серьезные последствия для наших дружеских отношений, нашей карьеры и самого нашего статуса в обществе.

Во всем мире в каждом обществе чистоплотности придается большое значение. Однако время от времени правительства решают потребовать от своего населения соблюдениz более высоких стандартов гигиены. Причиной иногда является восприятие опасности болезни, иногда - внешние угрозы, например война, а иногда - угрозы возникают для всей нации. Обеспокоенность относительно туберкулеза и гриппа в Европе 1920-х годов дала нам памятный лозунг "Кашель и чихание распространяют болезни". Художники периода Второй мировой войны - такие, как Эбрам Геймс в Соединенном Королевстве Великобритании и Северной Ирландии, - создали плакаты, иллюстрирующие "опасности грязи" и предупреждающие солдата о необходимости личной чистоплотности: "Ты обязан делать это для твоих же товарищей". В ходе послевоенного строительства пропагандировались такие культурные ценности, как бытовые туалеты, и в то же время экономический прогресс в более богатых странах дал мыло в каждую семью.

В 1950-е годы в Китае проведена первая серия патриотических кампаний в области гигиены. Соблюдение правил гигиены было обязанностью и буквально приравнивалось к выявлению вредителей, болезней и контрреволюционеров для построения нового Китая.

Несмотря на предпринятую деятельность, гигиена продолжает оставаться проблемой. Было установлено, что простое мытье рук с мылом может спасти более миллиона жизней в год. Пропаганда гигиены может быть одним из наиболее эффективных с точки зрения затрат средств достижения многих целей в области развития, связанных со здоровьем. Каким образом могут эти изображения научить нас тому, как поступать наилучшим образом? Плакаты, притягивающие взгляд, являются привлекательными, например аристократ со своим носовым платком, хорошенькие дети, моющие свои игрушки, птицы, чистящие зубы у крокодила. Изображения, которые мы запоминаем лучше всего, часто это те, которые сопровождаются простыми лозунгами, например, "не загрязняй бассейн" или "носовой платок спасает жизни". Ранние плакаты, нарисованные одним художником, выигрывают по сравнению с перегруженными, излишне сложными недавними изображениями, которые используют все символы графики на плакатах, сделанных группой художников. Но какие из этих изображений больше всего влияют на соблюдение правил гигиены? Истина состоит в том, что мы этого просто не знаем, и определение того, как наилучшим образом изменить поведение с помощью визуальных изображений, по-прежнему остается задачей, которую необходимо решить в 21-ом столетии.

保持清洁。 个人卫生是我们第二个免疫系统。它属于一整套几乎是不自觉的行为，可使我们远离污物、令人作呕并且带有危险的东西。个人卫生行为也是良好举止的体现。个人卫生与环境清洁得到父母、教师和领导的敦促、珍视和奖励。做的不好可对我们的友情、事业，甚至在社会中具有的地位带来严重影响。

世界上每个社会都高度重视清洁问题。可是，有时政府做出了决定，要求人们具备更高的卫生标准。究其原因，有时是由于感受到了疾病威胁，有时是遇到了外来威胁（如战争），有时是国家独立性遭受了威胁。20年代的欧洲对结核病和流感十分关切，我们就有了难以忘怀的口号：'咳嗽、打喷嚏，可传播疾病'。比如，英国的Abram Games等第二次世界大战艺术家制作了一些海报，展示'污物的危险'，告诫战士们注意个人清洁：'你应把它归功于你的伙伴'。战后国家在建筑方面推崇诸如室内厕所等文明价值观，同时较富裕国家的经济进步使得肥皂进入了每个家庭。

50年代，中国首先发起了一系列爱国卫生运动。为了建设一个新中国，遵守卫生规定成了一项义务，这确实是用来驱逐害虫、疾病和反革命分子。

尽管作了一个世纪的努力，个人卫生仍然是一个问题。据测算，用肥皂洗手这样的简单举止每年就可挽救100多万人的生命。讲究个人卫生可以成为实现许多卫生相关发展目标的最具成本效益的方式之一。这些图像可以教我们怎样做的更好呢？吸引眼球的海报才具有吸引力：一个贵族握着手帕，漂亮的孩子们正在清洗玩具，鳄鱼与鸟在一起。我们最容易记住的通常是哪些口号简单易懂的海报。可以是'泳池内杜绝污物'，或者是"一人及时使用手帕，能保护九人健康"。与能够显示委员会设计特征、既杂乱又极为复杂的近期图像相比，单个艺术家早期设计的海报更胜一筹。但是，哪些海报对个人卫生带来了最大影响呢？真实情况是，我们根本不知道。要了解怎样通过视觉图像更好地改变行为，仍是21世纪要完成的一项任务。

حافظوا على نظافتكم. إن التصحح هو جهازنا المناعي الثاني، وهو عبارة عن مجموعة من السلوكيات الغريزية تقريباً والتي تحدو بنا إلى أن نتجنب المواد القذرة والمقرفة والخطيرة. ويُعد السلوك التصححي من العادات الحميدة أيضاً. ويقوم كل من الوالدين والمعلمين والقادة بالحض على اتباع عادات النظافة الشخصية (التصحح) والحفاظ على نظافة البيئة وإعطاء جوائز ومكافآت على ذلك، وقد تترتب على أي تفويت في هذا الأمر عواقب وخيمة بالنسبة إلى علاقاتنا وحياتنا المهنية ووضعنا الحقيقي في المجتمع.

وكل مجتمعات العالم تعطي قيمة كبيرة للنظافة. ومع ذلك فإن الحكومات تقرر بين الفينة والفينة مطالبة سكان بلدانها بمعايير تصحح أعلى. ويرجع ذلك تارة إلى إدراك تهديد مرضي ما وتارة أخرى إلى تهديد محدق بالهوية الوطنية. وقد أسفرت الهواجس الخاصة بالسل والأنفلونزا في أوروبا في العشرينات من القرن العشرين عن وضع الشعار البارز «السعال والعطس ينشران الأمراض». وإبان الحرب العالمية الثانية وضع فنانون، مثل أبرام غيمز في المملكة المتحدة لبريطانيا العظمى وأيرلندا الشمالية، ملصقات إعلانية تظهر «أخطار القاذورات» وتحذر الجنود بشأن النظافة الشخصية. ومن أمثلة ذلك شعار «إنك مدين بذلك لجميع رفقاء السلاح». وشهدت عملية بناء الأمم بعد الحرب الدعاية إلى القيم المدنية، مثل إقامة المراحيض المنزلية، بينما أوصل في الوقت ذاته التقدم الاقتصادي في البلدان الأغنى الصابون إلى كل أسرة.

وشهدت الخمسينات من القرن العشرين أول سلسلة من حملات التصحح الوطنية في الصين. وكانت مراعاة قواعد التصحح واجبا ساعد بالفعل على القضاء على الهوام والأمراض وأنصار الثورة المضادة من أجل بناء صين جديدة.

وعلى الرغم من العمل طيلة قرن من الزمان مازال التصحح يُعد إحدى المشكلات. وكشفت التقديرات أن إجراءً بسيطاً كغسل اليدين بالصابون يمكن أن ينقذ أرواح مليون إنسان سنوياً. ويمكن أن يكون تعزيز التصحح من أكثر السُبل مردودية لتحقيق العديد من المرامي الإنمائية المتعلقة بالصحة. فما الذي يمكن أن نتعلمه من هذه الصور بشأن كيفية المُضي قدماً في هذا الصدد؟ إن الملصقات الإعلانية التي تجذب البصر هي الملصقات الإعلانية الأخاذة مثل صورة الأرستقراطي الذي يمسك بمنديله وصورة الأطفال الحسني المظهر وهم ينظفون لعبهم وصورة التمساح مع الطائر. إن الصور التي نتذكرها أكثر من غيرها هي في الغالب الصور ذات الشعارات البسيطة سواء أكانت من قبيل "حافظ على الترعة خالية من الأوساخ" أو "استعمال المنديل في الوقت المناسب يحمي تسعة". ويظل للملصقات الإعلانية الأولى التي صممها فنانون أفراد رونقها مقارنة بالصور الحديثة المختلطة والبالغة التعقيد التي تنم عن سابق إصرار من قبل اللجنة. ولكن ما هي الصور الأكثر تأثيراً من بينها في التصحح؟ الحقيقة أننا، وبكل بساطة، لا نعرف، ومازال تحري أفضل السُبل الكفيلة بتغيير السلوك عن طريق الصور مهمة مهمة لابد من إنجازها في القرن الحادي والعشرين.

■ Prevent infectious respiratory diseases. ■ Evitez les maladies respiratoires infectieuses. ■ Prevenga las infecciones respiratorias. ■ Предупреждайте инфекционные респираторные болезни.

■ عليكم بالوقاية من أمراض الجهاز التنفسي المعدية.

■ Where should you spit? In your handkerchief! Tissue paper! The spittoon!
■ Où cracher ? Dans ton mouchoir, dans un mouchoir en papier, dans le crachoir ! ■ ¿Dónde puedo escupir? Utilice un pañuelo de tela o de papel o un escupidero! ■ Куда плевать? В носовой платок! В бумажную салфетку! В плевательницу!

■ أين تبصقون؟ في المنديل ! أم في المنديل الورقي ! أم في المبصقة !

■ Please don't spit on the ground. Spitting on the ground is neither sanitary nor civilized. ■ Ne crache pas par terre. C'est un comportement contraire à l'hygiène et peu civilisé. ■ Absténgase de escupir en el piso. Es una costumbre antihigiénica y poco civilizada. ■ Не плюйте на землю! Плевать на землю негигиенично и некультурно.

■ الرجاء عدم البصق على الأرض. إن البصق على الأرض عادة غير صحية ولا حضارية.

JIANG JIU WEI SHENG YU FANG JI BING

■ Keep the baby's toy clean. ■ Le jouet de bébé doit être propre.
■ Mantenga limpios los juguetes de los niños. ■ Содержите
детские игрушки в чистоте.

■ حافظوا على نظافة لعب الأطفال.

从小讲卫生

■ Cleanliness helps to prevent diseases. ■ Une bonne hygiène contribue à
éviter les maladies. ■ Una buena higiene ayuda a prevenir enfermedades.
■ Санитарная гигиена помогает предотвращать болезни.

■ التصحح يساعد على الوقاية من الأمراض.

■ Hygienic habits start at a young age. ■ L'hygiène, cela s'apprend dès le plus jeune âge. ■ Los hábitos
sanitarios deben transmitirse desde la primera infancia. ■ Привычки соблюдать правила гигиены
вырабатываются в детстве.

■ العادات الصحية تبدأ منذ الصغر.

Why not wash your hands?

Protect the water you swim in and the health of those you swim with. Keep poop out of the pool by washing your hands.

Healthy Swimming
www.healthyswimming.org

■ Pourquoi ne vous lavez-vous pas les mains ? Adoptez de bonnes pratiques d'hygiène. Protégez l'eau dans laquelle vous nagez et la santé de ceux qui nagent à vos côtés.
■ ¿Por qué no se lava las manos? Proteja el agua en la que se bañe y la salud de quienes se bañen con usted. ■ Мойте руки. Обеспечивайте чистоту воды, в которой вы купаетесь, и здоровье тех, с которыми вы купаетесь. ■ 你为何不洗手？保护游泳池中的水和游泳同伴的健康。

■ لماذا لا تغسل يديك ؟ حافظ على نظافة الماء الذي تسبح فيه وعلى صحة من تسبح معهم.

■ Clean hands - Good. Mum is great, always guarding the family's health by ensuring hands are washed with soap. ■ Des mains propres - C'est bien. Maman veille toujours à la santé de sa famille en nous incitant à nous laver les mains avec du savon. ■ Las manos limpias, como debe ser. Mamá es fantástica : protege la salud de la familia haciendo que nos lavemos las manos con jabón. ■ Чистые руки – это хорошо. Мама всегда оберегает здоровье семьи и следит за тем, чтобы руки мыли с мылом. ■ 洁净的双手有好处。妈妈做的真好，她总是用肥皂洗手，保护家庭健康。

نظافة الأيدي أمر جيد. الأم العظيمة تحافظ دائماً على صحة أسرتها بغسل الأيدي بالصابون.

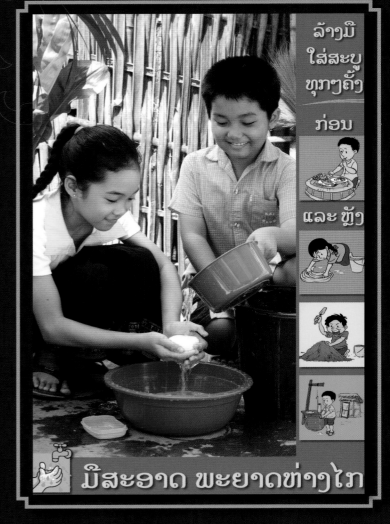

■ Don't let your hands make you ill. Wash your hands each time with soap. ■ Ne laisse pas tes mains te rendre malade : lave-toi les mains chaque fois avec du savon. ■ Que tus manos no te hagan enfermar. Lávatelas siempre con jabón. ■ Если не мыть руки, можно заболеть. Мойте руки каждый раз с мылом. ■ 请不要让你的双手带来疾病。每次都要用肥皂洗手。

■ لا تجعلوا أيديكم سبباً لإصابتكم بالمرض. اغسلوا أيديكم بالصابون دائماً.

■ Wash your hands before and after meals. Your hands will be clean, diseases will not affect you. ■ Lave-toi les mains avant et après le repas ! Ainsi elles seront propres et les maladies t'épargneront. ■ Lávate las manos antes y después de las comidas. Las manos limpias ahuyentarán las enfermedades. ■ Мойте руки до и после еды. Если руки будут чистыми, болезнь не пристанет к вам. ■ 饭前饭后要洗手。手干净了，就不易得病。

■ اغسلوا أيديكم قبل الأكل وبعده. ستبقى أيديكم نظيفة والأمراض بعيدة عنكم.

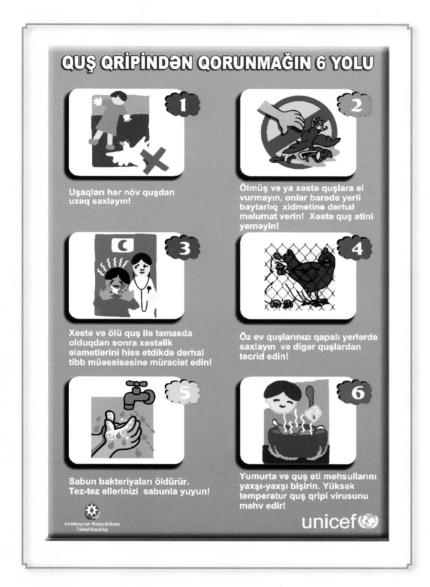

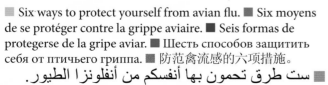

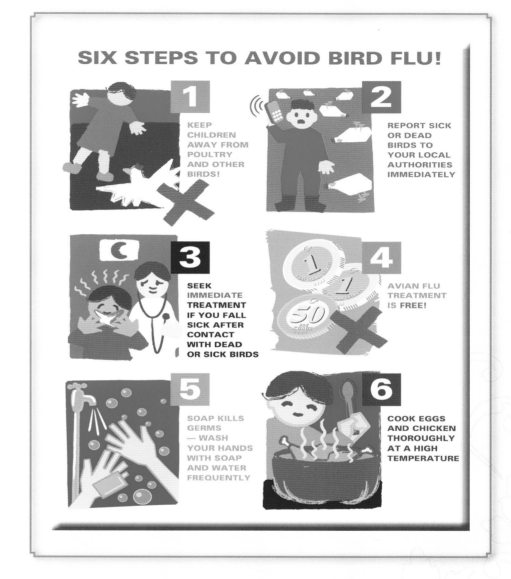

■ Six ways to protect yourself from avian flu. ■ Six moyens de se protéger contre la grippe aviaire. ■ Seis formas de protegerse de la gripe aviar. ■ Шесть способов защитить себя от птичьего гриппа. ■ 防范禽流感的六项措施。

■ ست طرق تحمون بها أنفسكم من أنفلونزا الطيور.

■ Six mesures pour éviter la grippe aviaire. ■ Seis medidas para prevenir la gripe aviar. ■ Шесть шагов для избежания птичьего гриппа. ■ 预防禽流感的六项措施。

■ ست خطوات لتجنب الإصابة بأنفلونزا الطيور.

■ Avian flu. Protect your children's health. Make sure they wash their hands with soap and water if they have been in contact with birds or poultry. Try to make sure they have as little contact as possible with them. ■ Grippe aviaire. Protégez la santé de vos enfants. Veillez à ce qu'ils se lavent les mains avec de l'eau et du savon s'ils ont été en contact avec des oiseaux et des volailles et à limiter de tels contacts dans la mesure du possible. ■ Gripe aviar. Proteja la salud de sus hijos. Compruebe que se laven las manos con agua y jabón si han estado en contacto con aves silvestres o de corral, y limite al máximo su contacto con ellas. ■ Птичий грипп. Защищайте здоровье ваших детей. Следите за тем, чтобы они мыли руки водой с мылом после контакта с дикими и домашними птицами, и, по возможности, ограничьте такие контакты. ■ 禽流感。保护儿童健康。如果他们接触了鸟类或家禽，一定要用肥皂和水洗手。尽量做到少接触鸟类和家禽。

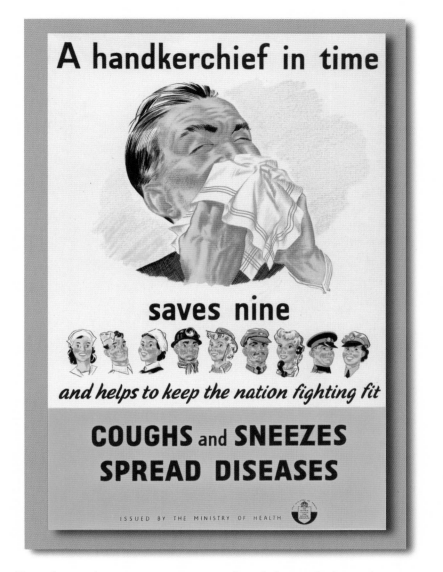

■ Eviter la maladie. En crachant, en toussant ou en éternuant sans faire attention, on risque de propager la grippe et la tuberculose. ■ Prevenga las infecciones. Escupir, toser o estornudar sin las debidas precauciones contribuye a propagar la gripe y la tuberculosis. ■ Предупреждайте болезни. Грипп и туберкулез распространяются с мокротой в результате кашля и чихания. ■ 预防疾病：随意吐痰、咳嗽、打喷嚏，可传播流感和结核病。
■ عليك بالوقاية من المرض: البصق والسعال والعطس بلا مبالاة عادات تنشر الأنفلونزا والسل.

■ Vite le mouchoir pour ne pas propager la maladie et aider le pays à rester en bonne santé. ■ Un pañuelo a tiempo puede proteger a muchas personas ... y ayudar a mantener en forma a la nación. ■ Употребив вовремя носовой платок, вы не заразите окружающих и поможете всей стране бороться с болезнями. ■ 及时使用手帕，能够保护多人，同时利于国家维系健康。
■ استعمال المنديل في الوقت المناسب يحمي تسعة ويساعد على أن تواصل الأمة مكافحة المرض على النحو الملائم.

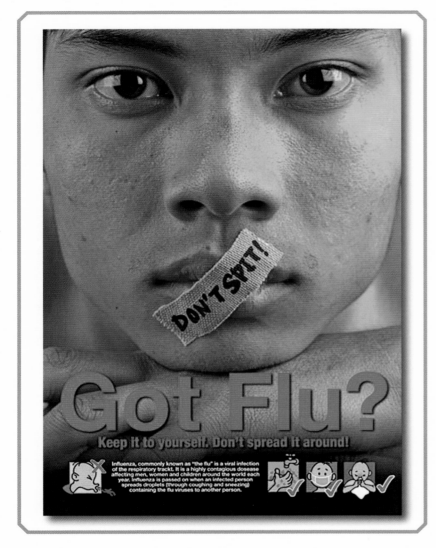

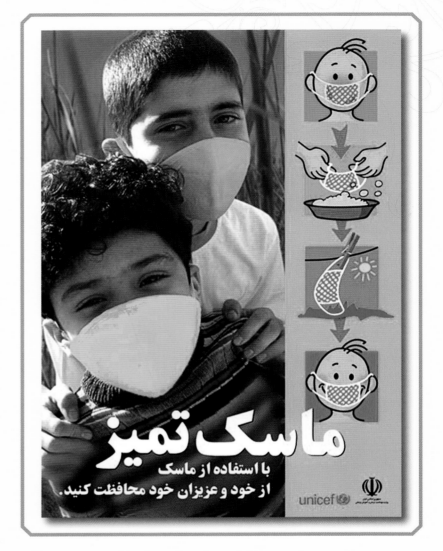

■ Ne crache pas. Tu es grippé ? Au moins ne propage pas tes virus.

■ ¡No escupas! ¿Griposo? Ten cuidado, no disperses el virus.

■ Не разбрызгивай слюну. Заболел гриппом? Держи его при себе, не распространяй вирусы вокруг себя. ■ 请勿吐痰。患流感了吗？影响你一人已经足够，请不要传给他人。

■ هل أنت مصاب بالأنفلونزا؟ لا تنقلها إلى غيرك ولا تنشرها من حولك.

■ Protect yourself and your loved ones by using a clean mask.

■ Se protéger et protéger sa famille en portant un masque propre.

■ Protégete y protege a los tuyos empleando una mascarilla limpia.

■ Стерильная маска. Защищайте себя и близких - надевайте маску.

■ 戴上洁净口罩，保护自己，也保护你珍爱的人们。

■ الكمامة النظيفة. احموا أنفسكم وأحباءكم بواسطة الكمامة.

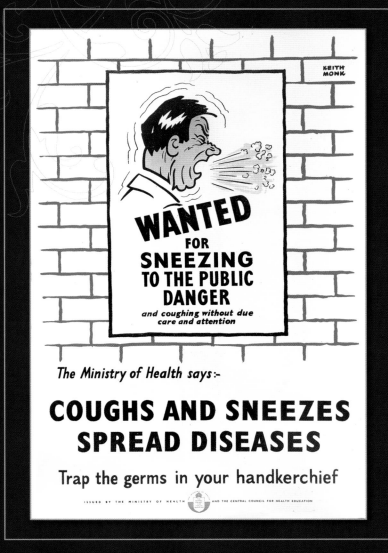

KEITH MONK

WANTED
FOR
SNEEZING
TO THE PUBLIC
DANGER
and coughing without due care and attention

The Ministry of Health says:-

COUGHS AND SNEEZES SPREAD DISEASES

Trap the germs in your handkerchief

ISSUED BY THE MINISTRY OF HEALTH AND THE CENTRAL COUNCIL FOR HEALTH EDUCATION

How much does a cold cost ?

Last year the common cold
and 'flu cost the country
40 million days' work
Don't be careless—Keep your
cold to yourself

COUGHS AND SNEEZES SPREAD DISEASES
Trap the germs in your handkerchief

ISSUED BY THE MINISTRY OF HEALTH

Printed for H.M. Stationery Office by Wm. Brown & Co., Ltd., London, E.C.3. 51-4254

■ En toussant et en éternuant, on propage des maladies.
■ La tos y los estornudos pueden propagar enfermedades.
■ Болезни распространяются через кашель и чихание.
■ 咳嗽、打喷嚏会传播疾病。
■ السعال والعطس ينشران الأمراض.

■ Combien coûte un rhume ? En toussant et en éternuant, on propage la maladie. ■ ¿Cuánto cuesta un resfriado? La tos y los estornudos pueden propagar enfermedades. ■ Сколько стоит простуда? Болезни распространяются через кашель и чихание. ■ 一次感冒花费多少？咳嗽、打喷嚏传播疾病。
■ ما تكلفة الإصابة بالبرد؟ السعال والعطس ينشران الأمراض.

contre la carie!

Les pommes aident à nettoyer les dents et massent les gencives, la meilleure recette pour des dents saines: croquez une pomme chaque jour à dix heures et à quatre heures.

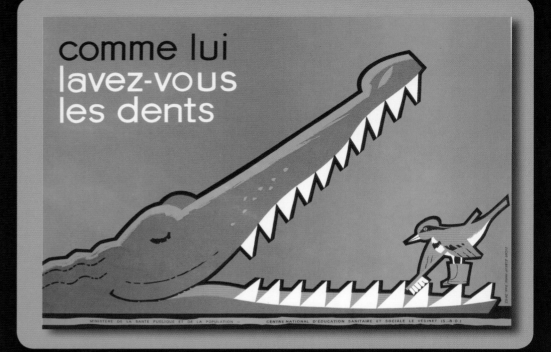

comme lui lavez-vous les dents

MINISTÈRE DE LA SANTÉ PUBLIQUE ET DE LA POPULATION — CENTRE NATIONAL D'ÉDUCATION SANITAIRE ET SOCIALE LE VÉSINET (S.-B.-O.)

■ Like him, brush your teeth. ■ Siga su ejemplo: cepíllese los dientes. ■ Чистите зубы, как и он. ■ 像他一样刷牙。

■ اغسلوا أسنانكم مثله.

■ Fight dental caries! ■ ¡Combatamos la caries! ■ Что лучше против кариеса! ■ 抗击龋齿！

■ كافحوا تسوس الأسنان!

■ Toute habitation doit avoir une installation sanitaire.
■ Su hogar no está completo sin un módulo sanitario.
■ Ваш дом – не дом, если в нем нет туалета. ■ 缺少卫生
设施，你的居家就不完美。

■ منزلك لا يكتمل بناؤه إذا لم يجهز بوحدة إصحاح.

■ Mise en échec par l'assainissement communautaire. La planification de l'assainissement empêche les mouches d'avoir accès à des agents pathogènes mortels. ■ Otra víctima del saneamiento comunitario. Los planes de saneamiento comunitario mantienen las moscas alejadas de gérmenes mortales. ■ Перехитрим заразу. Санитария в общине отгоняет мух от смертельных зародышей болезней. ■ 社区环境卫生可以智胜疾病。规划完好的社区环境卫生设施可使苍蝇远离致命病菌。

■ الإصحاح في المجتمع المحلي يقهر الذباب. تخطيط الإصحاح في المجتمع المحلي يبعد الذباب دائماً عن جراثيم الأمراض الفتاكة.

常洗衣被常洗澡,保持清潔身體好

Help your neighborhood by keeping your premises clean

TENEMENT HOUSE DEPT.
OF THE CITY OF NEW YORK

F. H. LAGUARDIA
MAYOR

LANGDON W. POST
COMMISSIONER

■ To keep yourself clean and healthy regularly wash your clothes and bed sheets and bathe often. ■ Pour rester propre et en bonne santé il faut laver ses vêtements et ses draps et se baigner souvent. ■ Para conservarse limpio y con buena salud, hay que lavar con frecuencia la ropa y las sábanas, y bañarse a menudo. ■ Как можно чаще чистите

■ Aidez le voisinage en préservant la propreté chez vous. ■ Ayude a su vecindario: cuide la higiene de su local o vivienda. ■ Если в вашем доме чисто – это поможет и соседям. ■ 保持居家清洁，为邻居带来帮助。

Make every day a healthy day
• protect yourself • protect others

Emerging Infectious Diseases

World Health Day, 7 April, 1997

THE FLY IS AS DEADLY AS A BOMBER!!

PHILADELPHIA DEPARTMENT OF PUBLIC HEALTH

■ Que chaque jour soit un jour de santé. Protégez–vous, protégez autrui.
■ Haga de cada día un día saludable. Protéjase a sí mismo y a quienes le rodean.
■ Сделай каждый день здоровым днем. Защити себя. Защити других.
■ 健康充满每一天。保护你自己，也保护他人。
■ اجعلوا من كل يوم يوم صحة عالمياً ـ احموا أنفسكم واحموا الآخرين.

■ La mouche sème la mort autant qu'un bombardier ! ■ Una mosca puede ser tan mortífera como un bombardero. ■ Муха так же опасна, как и бомба. ■ 苍蝇如同炸弹一样具有危害！

الذبابة لا تقل فتكاً عن قاذفة القنابل!

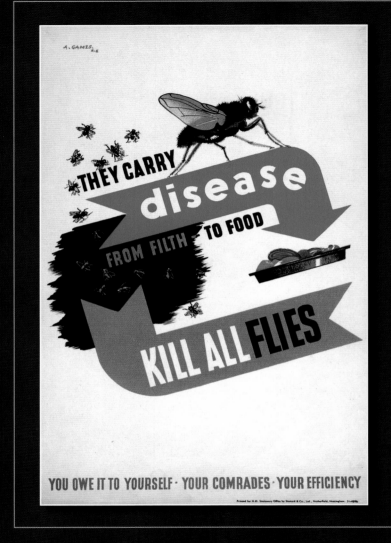

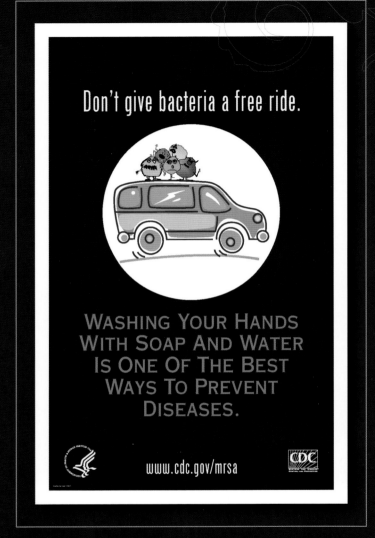

■ Elles transportent la maladie de la saleté aux aliments. Mort aux mouches !
■ Así se transmiten las enfermedades de la inmundicia a la comida. ¡Mate todas las moscas! ■ Мухи переносят болезни из грязи в пищу. Убей всех мух. ■ 它们把疾病从肮脏之处带入食物。把苍蝇灭光。

■ الذباب يحمل المرض من القاذورات إلى الطعام. اقتلوا كل الذباب.

■ Ne prends pas les bactéries en autostop. Lave-toi les mains avec de l'eau et du savon, c'est un des meilleurs moyens d'éviter la maladie. ■ No saque las bacterias de paseo. Lavarse las manos con agua y jabón es uno de los mejores modos de prevenir enfermedades. ■ Не предоставляйте бактериям бесплатный проезд. Мытье рук водой с мылом – один из лучших способов предотвратить болезни. ■ 不要让细菌自由搭车。用肥皂和水洗手，是防病的一个最佳方式

■ لا تعط الجراثيم توصيلة مجانية. غسل يديك بالصابون والماء من أفضل
ق الوقاية من الأمراض.

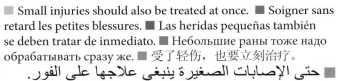

■ Small injuries should also be treated at once. ■ Soigner sans retard les petites blessures. ■ Las heridas pequeñas también se deben tratar de inmediato. ■ Небольшие раны тоже надо обрабатывать сразу же. ■ 受了轻伤，也要立刻治疗。

■ حتى الإصابات الصغيرة ينبغي علاجها على الفور.

■ Restez propre. ■ Cuide su higiene. ■ Соблюдай чистоту! ■ 保持清洁。

■ حافظ على نظافتك.

Protegerse

Protect yourself

Берегите себя

Se protéger

عليكم بحماية أنفسكم

保护健康

Protect yourself. The discovery of methods to mass-produce penicillin in the 1940s changed medicine forever. For the first time in history, we had an effective means to treat infectious diseases such as syphilis. Poster campaigns reflected this victory, promising the general public that complete cures were at hand. At the same time, to compel responsible sexual behaviour, the posters drew strategically on long-standing fears surrounding sexual activity. Avoidance, after all, was the most effective protection against sexually transmitted diseases (STDs). Avoiding prostitutes, in particular, was advocated; for they were seen both as the source of actual infection and the root of the moral and social decay that threatened the very foundations of family life and prosperity. It is hardly surprising therefore that during the Second World War, with men at the front and women alone at home, the production of these kinds of stigmatizing posters soared.

The appearance of the acquired immunodeficiency syndrome (AIDS) in the United States of America in the 1980s radically challenged public health campaigns about STDs. Not least, this was because there was no definitive cure at hand. Moreover, although sex was the predominant mode of transmitting the human immunodeficiency virus (HIV) which can cause AIDS, it was not the only means; drug users and those requiring blood transfusions were also at high risk. Partly because of this, but more importantly because many cultures had adopted far more liberal attitudes to sexuality and sexual difference, HIV/AIDS poster campaigns avoided putting blame on particular social groups in the way that campaigns for other STDs had done in the past.

Unsurprisingly, older themes visible in the STD campaigns of 60 years before re-emerged, for example through the use of religious iconography, and images of pregnant women and innocent children. Eventually, the campaigns moved beyond the fear factor, often reflecting changes in lifestyles and sexual mores. This is evident for example, in posters depicting confident women making their own choices about sexual protection and celebrating condoms as the best way to avoid infection.

Whereas avoiding risky sex had often been the instruction of earlier STD campaigns, the message now was to act as a responsible sexual adult by using a condom. Hence, at the same time that new HIV/AIDS charities took over many educational functions from national departments of health, commercial condom manufacturers also entered the public health arena, promising protection through the use of their products. Distancing itself from its image as an amoral icon, the condom moved centre stage in campaigns against HIV/AIDS in many countries. Elsewhere however, local mores, local customs in health education and local aesthetic traditions have been preserved in the enduring battle that has united the world in preventive practices against HIV/AIDS.

Se protéger. La mise au point de méthodes de production de masse de la pénicilline dans les années 40 a transformé la médecine. Pour la première fois, on disposait d'un moyen efficace pour traiter des maladies comme la syphilis. Des campagnes d'affiches ont reflété cette victoire, promettant au grand public la perspective d'une guérison complète. Parallèlement, pour inciter les gens à adopter un comportement sexuel responsable, les affiches revenaient sur les craintes à long terme liées à l'activité sexuelle. L'abstinence n'est-elle pas après tout la protection la plus efficace contre les maladies sexuellement transmissibles (MST) ? On préconisait notamment de ne pas fréquenter la prostituée considérée comme la source tant d'une contamination physique que d'une dégradation morale et sociale menaçant la survie de la vie familiale et de la prospérité. Il ne faut donc pas s'étonner de la prolifération de ces affiches moralisatrices pendant la deuxième guerre mondiale à l'époque où le mari était au front et la femme seule au foyer.

L'apparition du syndrome d'immunodéficience acquise aux Etats-Unis d'Amérique dans les années 80 a conduit à une remise en question radicale des campagnes de santé publique relatives aux MST, en grande partie parce qu'on se trouvait sans moyen de guérir le nouveau fléau. En outre, même s'il était le principal mode de transmission du virus de l'immunodéficience humaine – agent responsable du sida – , le sexe n'était pas le seul puisque toxicomanes et transfusés étaient également exposés. En partie pour cela, mais aussi – ce qui est plus important – parce que nombre de cultures avaient adopté des attitudes bien plus libérales, les campagnes d'affiches concernant le VIH/sida ont évité de montrer du doigt des groupes sociaux particuliers comme on l'avait fait jadis pour d'autres MST.

Il n'est pas étonnant de voir alors resurgir les thèmes empruntés à des campagnes vieilles de 60 ans sur les MST, par exemple avec un recours à l'iconographie religieuse ou à des images de femmes enceintes et d'enfants innocents. Puis, on a dépassé le stade de la peur, en reflétant souvent les modifications des modes de vies et des coutumes sexuelles : en témoignent les affiches montrant des femmes sûres d'elles faisant leur propre choix pour se protéger et considérant le préservatif comme le meilleur moyen d'éviter l'infection.

Dans les précédentes campagnes concernant les MST, il s'agissait d'éviter le sexe à risque ; cette fois, le message était d'agir de façon responsable en utilisant le préservatif. Ainsi, alors même que de nouvelles associations bénévoles reprenaient les activités d'éducation concernant le VIH/sida aux départements nationaux de la santé, les fabricants de préservatifs faisaient également leur entrée dans l'arène de la santé publique en promettant la protection de leur produit. S'éloignant de cette image d'icône amorale, le préservatif a ainsi fait irruption en plein milieu des campagnes de lutte contre le VIH/sida dans nombre de pays. Mais il est vrai qu'ailleurs, les coutumes et habitudes locales en matière d'éducation pour la santé et de bienséance ont été préservées dans la lutte durable qui a uni les pays du monde entier en faveur de la prévention du VIH/sida.

Protegerse. La puesta a punto de métodos de producción penicilina en gran escala en los años cuarenta cambió para siempre el panorama de la medicina. Por primera vez en la historia, se disponía de un medio eficaz para tratar enfermedades como la sífilis. Las campañas realizadas con carteles reflejaban esa victoria, pues prometían a la población que había una curación completa al alcance. Paralelamente, para forzar a adoptar un comportamiento sexual responsable, los carteles recurrían estratégicamente a los temores que siempre han rodeado a la actividad sexual. La abstinencia, al fin y al cabo, era la forma más eficaz de protección contra las enfermedades de transmisión sexual (ETS). Se exhortaba a evitar en particular a las prostitutas, consideradas a la vez fuente de infección y causa del declive moral y social que amenazaba los fundamentos mismos de la vida familiar y la prosperidad. No es de extrañar por tanto que durante la Segunda Guerra Mundial, con los hombres en el frente y las mujeres solas en casa, la producción de esos carteles estigmatizadores se disparase.

La aparición en los Estados Unidos de América del síndrome de inmunodeficiencia adquirida (sida) durante los años ochenta imprimió un giro radical a las campañas de salud pública centradas en las ETS, en buena parte por el hecho de que no se disponía de ninguna medida curativa contra él. Además, las relaciones sexuales constituían la principal vía de transmisión del virus del sida, pero no la única; los consumidores de drogas y las personas que necesitaban transfusiones de sangre también estaban expuestos a ese riesgo. En parte a causa de ello, pero sobre todo porque muchas culturas se habían vuelto considerablemente más liberales en lo relativo a la sexualidad, las campañas con carteles sobre el VIH/sida evitaban censurar a ningún grupo social en particular, como se había hecho en otras campañas anteriores contra distintas ETS.

No es de extrañar que reaparecieran temas de campañas emprendidas contra las ETS 60 años antes, como por ejemplo imágenes religiosas o de mujeres embarazadas y niños inocentes. Finalmente las campañas superaron el factor miedo, en consonancia con la evolución de los modos de vida y de las costumbres sexuales. Ello es evidente, por ejemplo, en los carteles que muestran a mujeres seguras de sí mismas tomando sus propias decisiones sobre la protección sexual y promoviendo los preservativos como opción idónea para no sufrir infecciones.

Evitar las relaciones sexuales de riesgo fue una recomendación frecuente en las primeras campañas contra las ETS, pero luego el mensaje se centró en actuar como adultos sexualmente responsables usando el preservativo. Por ello, al tiempo que nuevas organizaciones de beneficencia contra el VIH/sida asumían muchas funciones de educación de los ministerios nacionales de salud, numerosos fabricantes comerciales de preservativos empezaron a actuar también en el campo de la salud pública, prometiendo protección gracias a la utilización de sus productos. Alejándose de esa imagen de icono amoral, el preservativo pasó a ser el principal protagonista de las campañas contra el VIH/sida en muchos países. En otras partes, sin embargo, se han mantenido las normas y costumbres locales en materia de educación sanitaria y las tradiciones estéticas locales en esta larga batalla que ha unido al mundo en las prácticas preventivas contra el VIH/sida.

Берегите себя. Открытие методов массового производства пенициллина в 1940-е годы навсегда изменило медицину. Впервые в истории мы получили эффективное средство для лечения инфекционных болезней, таких как сифилис. Плакатная кампания отражает эту победу, обещая населению, что полное излечение возможно. В то же время для стимулирования ответственного сексуального поведения плакаты играли на давних страхах, связанных с половой активностью. Избежание, в конечном счете, было самой эффективной защитой от болезней, передаваемых половым путем. В частности, пропагандировалось избегать проституток, так как они считались как источником реальных инфекций, так и коренной причиной морального и социального падения, угрожавшего самим основам семейной жизни и процветания. Поэтому вряд ли удивительно, что во время Второй мировой войны, когда мужчины были на фронте, а женщины остались дома одни, производство такого рода клеймящих позором плакатов стремительно увеличилось.

Появление синдрома приобретенного иммунодефицита (СПИДа) в Соединенных Штатах Америки в середине 1980-х годов резко изменило кампании общественного здравоохранения в отношении БППП. Не в последнюю очередь это произошло из-за отсутствия возможности полного излечения. Кроме того, хотя секс и был основным видом передачи вируса иммунодефицита человека (ВИЧ), который может вызывать СПИД, он был не единственным; высокому риску подвергались также наркоманы и люди, нуждавшиеся в переливании крови. Отчасти из-за этого, но также, что более важно, из-за того, что во многих культурных условиях отношение к сексуальности и сексуальным различиям стало более либеральным, кампании с плакатами против ВИЧ/СПИДа избегали порицания конкретных социальных групп таким образом, как это делали кампании против других БППП в прошлом.

Неудивительно, что на плакатах вновь появились темы, использовавшиеся в кампаниях против БППП 60-летней давности, например религиозные изображения и изображения беременной женщины и невинного младенца. В конечном счете кампании преодолели это фактор страха, отражая зачастую изменения в образе жизни и сексуальных нормах. Это видно, например, на плакатах, изображающих уверенную женщину, которая делает свой выбор относительно сексуальной защиты, и прославляющих презервативы как наилучший способ защиты от инфекций.

Если избежание рискованного секса часто было инструкцией более ранних кампаний против БППП, то сейчас сообщение состоит в том, чтобы действовать по-взрослому ответственно и использовать презерватив. Поэтому одновременно с тем, что новые учреждения по борьбе против ВИЧ/СПИДа взяли на себя у департаментов здравоохранения многие просветительские функции, на арену общественного здравоохранения вышли коммерческие производители презервативов, обещая защиту с помощью использования своей продукции. Дистанцируясь от своего имиджа, во многих странах презерватив из аморального символа превратился в объект, занимающий центральное место в кампаниях против ВИЧ/СПИДа. Вместе с тем, повсеместно местные нравы, местные традиции медико-санитарного просвещения и местные эстетические принципы сохранились в трудной борьбе, которая объединяет мир для предупреждения ВИЧ/СПИДа.

保护健康。 上世纪40年代，青霉素的发明使医学发生了永久性变化。在历史上，医学首次具备了能够有效治疗梅毒等传染病的手段。海报的宣传活动体现了这一成就，公众看到疾病的完全治愈就在眼前。同时，为了迫使人们对性行为负责，海报从战略上利用了长期以来人们在性活动上存有的疑虑。回避毕竟是预防性病的最有效方式。特别是鼓励人们要避开妓女，这时因为妓女既被看作疾病的实际感染源，又被当作道德和社会腐化的根源，这对家庭生活和繁荣根基带来了威胁。因此，在第二次世界大战期间，男人在前线，女人独自在家，制作这类带有耻辱性的海报能够风行一时也就不足为奇了。

80年代，艾滋病在美国的出现对性病的公共卫生宣传活动带来了彻底的挑战。这并不仅是因为当前没有根本性治愈办法。另外，尽管性行为是疾病传播的主要方式，但并不是唯一的方式：吸毒者和需要输血者，同样具有高度危险。这只是部分原因，更重要的原因则是，许多文化对性活动和性行为差异持有更加开放的态度。在针对其它性病的宣传活动对特定社会人群提出责备的时候，艾滋病的海报宣传活动回避了这样的责备。

不足为奇，60年前见到的在性病宣传活动方面的古老主题又重新出现，例如利用宗教的图示法，以及孕妇和无辜儿童的图像加以宣传。最后，宣传活动超越了恐惧因素，常常反映出生活方式和性风俗的变化。比如，一些海报描述胸有成竹的妇女，选择自己的性活动保护方法，并宣称避免感染的最佳方式是使用安全套。

然而，避免危险性行为常常是早期性病宣传活动的行动指南，现在在宣传的主题内容为：使用安全套，做一名负责任的性活动成年人。因此，在一些新型艾滋病毒/艾滋病慈善机构取代了国家卫生部门的许多宣教职能的同时，安全套生产商也踏入了公共卫生领域，他们承诺通过销售产品实现保护健康。作为非道德范畴的指号，安全套在许多国家走向了艾滋病毒/艾滋病宣传活动的舞台中央。但在其它地方，当地民德、健康教育的当地风俗和当地审美习惯在这项长期斗争中得以保存下来，这个斗争已经使得世界团结起来，采取预防措施，防控艾滋病毒/艾滋病。

عليكم بحماية أنفسكم. إن اكتشاف طرق إنتاج البنسلين بكميات كبيرة في الأربعينات من القرن العشرين أحدث تغيراً في الطب سيستمر إلى الأبد. فللمرة الأولى في تاريخ الطب أصبحت لدينا وسيلة ناجعة لعلاج الأمراض المعدية، مثل الزهري. وقد جسدت الحملات التي استعملت الملصقات الإعلانية هذا النصر، وبشرت عامة الجمهور بإمكانية الشفاء التام. وقد كانت الملصقات تعتمد في الوقت نفسه وبشكل استراتيجي على المخاوف القديمة العهد التي تكتنف النشاط الجنسي وذلك من أجل الدفع في اتجاه السلوك الجنسي المسؤول. وكان التجنب، على الرغم من كل شيء، أنجع وسيلة للحماية من الأمراض المنقولة جنسياً. وكانت الدعوة موجهة بوجه خاص إلى تجنب العاهرات، حيث كان يُنظر إليهن على أنهن مصدر العدوى الفعلي وسبب التدهور الأخلاقي والاجتماعي الذي يهدد الأسس ذاتها التي تقوم عليها الحياة الأسرية. ومن ثم لم يكن من المدهش أن يتصاعد إنتاج هذا النوع من الملصقات الإعلانية أثناء الحرب العالمية الثانية حيث كان الرجال على الجبهة والنساء وحدهن في المنزل.

وتمخض ظهور مرض الأيدز في الولايات المتحدة الأمريكية في منتصف الثمانينات من القرن العشرين عن تحديات كبرى صادفت حملات الصحة العمومية في ما يتعلق بالأمراض المنقولة جنسياً. وما كان ذلك إلا نتيجة لعدم وجود أي علاج جذري. وبالإضافة إلى ذلك فعلى الرغم من أن ممارسة الجنس هي أول طريقة لنقل فيروس العوز المناعي البشري (فيروس الايدز) الذي يمكن أن يسبب الايدز فإنها لم تكن الطريقة الوحيدة، حيث إن الأشخاص الذين يتعاطون المخدرات والأشخاص الذين يحتاجون إلى نقل الدم كانوا أيضاً معرضين لمخاطر داهمة. وكان هذا أحد الأسباب التي جعلت حملات مكافحة الأيدز والعدوى بفيروسه التي تستعمل الملصقات الإعلانية تتجنب إلقاء اللوم على فئات اجتماعية معينة بالطريقة ذاتها التي اتبعتها حملات معنية بأمراض أخرى منقولة جنسياً في الماضي، وكان السبب الأهم في هذا التوجه هو أن هناك ثقافات عديدة اعتمدت مواقف أكثر تحرراً بكثير إزاء الجنس والفروق الجنسية.

ولا غرو أن المواضيع الأقدم التي ظهرت في حملات مكافحة الأمراض المنقولة جنسياً قبل أن تعاود الظهور، على سبيل المثال باستخدام الأيقونات ذات الطابع الديني وصور الحوامل والأطفال الأبرياء. وفي خاتمة المطاف تحولت الحملات عن عامل الخوف الذي كان يعكس في أغلب الأحوال التغيرات الطارئة على أنماط الحياة والميول الجنسية. ويتضح هذا مثلاً في الملصقات الإعلانية التي تبين المرأة الواثقة من نفسها وهي تتخذ اختياراتها الخاصة بشأن الحماية أثناء ممارسة الجنس، مع الاحتفاء بالعازل الذكري كأفضل وسيلة لتجنب الإصابة بالعدوى.

وفي حين أن تجنب المجازفة في ممارسة الجنس كان يُشكل موضوع الحملات المبكرة لمكافحة الأمراض المنقولة جنسياً فإن الرسالة التي يراد تبليغها الآن هي التصرف كشخص بالغ يمارس الجنس ويستعمل العازل الذكري. وبناءً على ذلك، وفي الوقت الذي أصبحت فيه المؤسسات الخيرية الجديدة المعنية بالأيدز والعدوى بفيروسه تقوم بالعديد من وظائف التوعية بدلاً من الإدارات الصحية الوطنية دخلت الشركات التجارية المنتجة للعازل الذكري أيضاً مجال الصحة العمومية، وبشرت بتوفير الحماية بفضل استخدام منتجاتها. وأصبح العازل الذكري، بعد أن كان رمزاً للتحلل الأخلاقي، محور اهتمام حملات مكافحة الأيدز والعدوى بفيروسه في كثير من البلدان. بيد أن هناك أماكن أخرى حوفظ فيها على الأخلاقيات والأعراف المحلية في مجال التوعية الصحية، وبقيت التقاليد الجمالية المحلية في المعركة الطاحنة التي جمعت العالم على الممارسات الوقائية لمكافحة الأيدز والعدوى بفيروسه.

■ La syphilis, une maladie qui existe depuis la nuit des temps est désormais guérissable: consulte ton médecin. ■ Una amenaza desde el principio de los tiempos. La sífilis ahora tiene curación. Consulte a su médico. ■ Такая старая болезнь, как сифилис, сейчас излечима. Проконсультируйтесь с врачом. ■ 与天地一样古老的梅毒，现在可以治愈：请去看医生。
■ الزهري، وهو المرض القديم قدم الخليقة، يمكن الشفاء منه الآن: استشر طبيبك.

■ Vive la mariée ! Le porteur d'une maladie vénérienne qui infecte son épouse commet un crime contre elle et ses enfants à naître. ■ Ahí va la novia. Un hombre con una enfermedad venérea que contagia a su esposa comete un crimen contra ésta y también contra sus futuros hijos. ■ Да здравствует новобрачная! Мужчина, страдающий от венерического заболевания и заразивший свою супругу, совершает ужасное преступление по отношению к ней и еще нерожденному ребенку. ■ 新娘来了！患有性病的男人，一旦传染给了妻子，对她和未来的孩子都是可耻的罪过。
■ مرحباً بالعروس. الرجل المصاب بمرض منقول جنسياً وينقل العدوى الى زوجته يرتكب جريمة بغيضة في حقها وفي حق ولدها القادم

■ Elle risque d'être une source de problèmes ... ■ Esta mujer puede ser un foco de problemas. ■ Она может быть источником … больших неприятностей. ■ 她可能会带来一大堆麻烦。

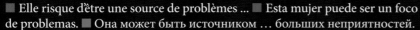

■ Elle peut avoir l'air propre – mais … ■ Puede que parezca limpia, pero… ■ На вид она здорова, но… ■ 看起来她未沾染疾病，但是⋯⋯。

قد تبدو نظيفة ولكن...

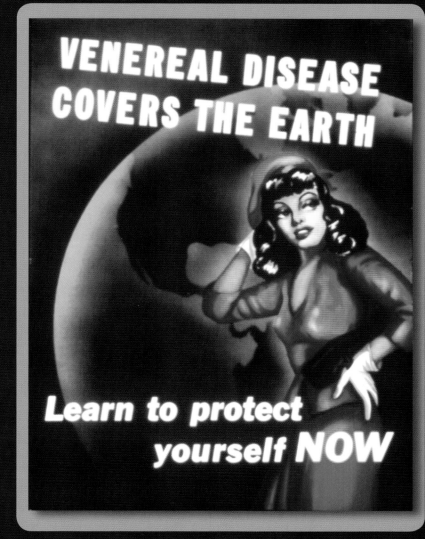

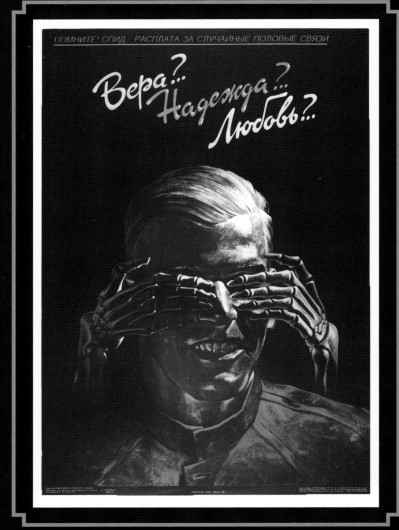

■ In order to keep healthy, avoid casual partners. ■ Pour préserver ta santé, évite les partenaires occasionnelles. ■ Proteja su salud: evite los contactos sexuales ocasionales. ■ 维护你的健康，远离临时性伴。

■ كي تحمي نفسك تجنب الضجيع الذي لا تعرفه.

■ Faith? Hope? Love? ■ Foi? Espérance? Amour? ■ ¿Fe? ¿Esperanza? ¿Amor? ■ 信念？希望？爱恋？

■ إيمان؟ أمل؟ حب؟

■ Mon petit ami m'a flanqué le sida. Moi, j'avais juste peur de tomber enceinte … ■ Mi novio me contagió el sida. Antes lo único que me preocupaba era el riesgo de quedarme embarazada. ■ Мой парень заразил меня СПИДом. А я боялась только забеременеть. ■ 我的艾滋病是由男友传染的。我只担心怀孕。

■ رفيقي نقل لي عدوى الأيدز. ولم يكن يعنيني إلا منع الحمل.

■ N'oublie pas le chapitre sur le sida. ■ No se salte el capítulo sobre el sida. ■ Занимаясь половым воспитанием, не забудь главу о СПИДе. ■ 艾滋病这一课，不能忘。

■ لا تنس الفصل الخاص بالأيدز.

 Evitez le sida, utilisez le préservatif. ■ Evita el sida, usa el preservativo.
■ Предотвращайте СПИД – используйте презерватив. ■ 避免艾滋
病，请用安全套。

 Tu as des capotes!? Oui, je me respecte. Ma santé est importante pour
moi. Ça ne devrait pas te surprendre. ■ ¿Llevas condones? Sí. Me respeto
y me preocupo por mi salud. ¿Qué hay de extraño en eso? ■ Ты носишь

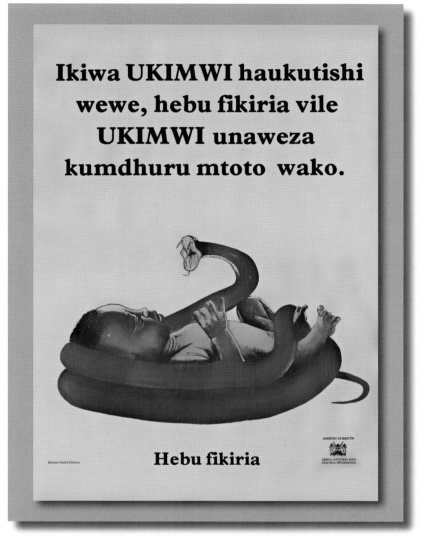

■ Si tu trouves que ça a l'air dangereux, essaie seulement d'en faire autant sans préservatif. ■ Si esto le parece peligroso, intente hacerlo sin preservativo. ■ Вам это кажется опасным? Опаснее без презерватива. ■ 你认为这样存有危险，不用避孕套才危险呢。

■ إذا كنت تعتقد أن هذا يبدو خطيراً فما عليك إلا أن تجرب فعله دون عازل ذكري.

■ If you're not afraid of what AIDS can do to you, think of what it can do to your baby. ■ Si tu n'as pas peur de ce que le sida peut te faire à toi, songe à ce qu'il peut faire à ton enfant. ■ Protéjase contra el sida: si no por su propio bien, por el bien de su bebé. ■ Если вы не боитесь СПИДа, подумайте, что он может сделать с вашим ребенком. ■ 如果你不惧怕艾滋病对你带来的影响，那就想想对你宝宝的影响吧。

■ إذا كنت لا تخشى ما يمكن أن يفعله بك الأيدز فكر في ما يمكن أن يفعله بوليدك.

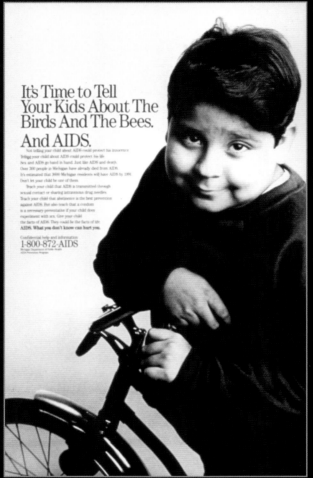

It's Time to Tell Your Kids About The Birds And The Bees. And AIDS.

Not telling your child about AIDS could protect his innocence. Telling your child about AIDS could protect his life. Sex and AIDS go hand in hand. Just like AIDS and death. Over 300 people in Michigan have already died from AIDS. It's estimated that 3000 Michigan residents will have AIDS by 1991. Don't let your child be one of them.

Teach your child that AIDS is transmitted through sexual contact or sharing intravenous drug needles. Teach your child that abstinence is the best prevention against AIDS. But also teach that a condom is a necessary preventative if your child does experiment with sex. Give your child the facts of life: AIDS. What you don't know can hurt you.

Confidential help and information.
1-800-872-AIDS
Michigan Department of Public Health
AIDS Prevention Program

Tes enfants grandissent. C'est le moment de leur parler des choses de la vie … et du sida. ■ Ha llegado el momento de explicarles a sus hijos de dónde vienen los niños. Y también el sida. ■ Настало время рассказать вашему ребенку, откуда берутся дети. Не забудьте рассказать и про СПИД. ■ 该把两性关系以及艾滋病的基本知识，告知你的孩子了。

Take This Vision Test

A

LOOK

TO 1991 SHOWS

270,000 PEOPLE WITH AIDS.

365,000 BY 1992. 465,000 BY 1993.

YOU CAN SEE AIDS MUST BE STOPPED NOW IF THE

NUMBER OF PEOPLE WITH AIDS IS TO GROW SMALLER AND SMALLER AND SMALLER.

Learn the facts about AIDS today. Pass them on.

 AIDS

Call 273-AIDS. Outside Milwaukee, 1-800-334-AIDS.

Figures from U.S. Public Health Service

If You're Dabbling In Drugs... You Could Be Dabbling With Your Life.

Skin popping, on occasion, seems a lot safer than mainlining. Right? You ask yourself. What can happen? Well, a lot can happen. That's because there's a new game in town. It's called AIDS. So far there are no winners. If you share needles, you're at risk. All it takes is one exposure to the AIDS virus and you've just dabbled your life away.

For more information about AIDS, call 1-800-342-AIDS.

AMERICA RESPONDS TO AIDS

■ Jouer avec la drogue, c'est jouer avec sa vie. ■ Jugar con las drogas… jugar con la muerte. ■ Если вы балуетесь наркотиками, вы рискуете своей жизнью. ■ 如果你在吸食毒品，你就可能在戏弄生命。

■ إذا كنت تلهو بالمخدرات فأنت تلعب بحياتك.

■ Passez ce test d'acuité visuelle. ■ Sométase a esta prueba de visión. ■ Проверьте ваше зрение. ■ 做一下这项视力测试。

■ جرب فحص النظر هذا.

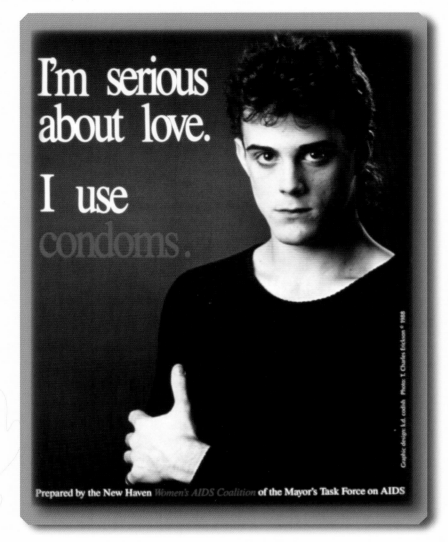

■ L'amour c'est sérieux pour moi. J'utilise le préservatif. ■ Para mí, el amor es algo serio. Yo utilizo preservativos. ■ К любви я отношусь серьезно. Я использую презерватив. ■ 我认真对待爱。我使用安全套。

■ أنا جاد في الحب. إنني استعمل العازل الذكري.

■ Le sida existe. Et quand tu lui parleras des choses de la vie, n'oublie pas ce principe capital : le préservatif permet une sexualité sans risques. ■ El sida es una realidad. Déle la importancia que se merece dentro de la educación sexual de su hija. Utilizar preservativos es apostar por la seguridad. ■ СПИД – это неопровержимый факт. Занимаясь половым воспитанием, не забудьте про самое важное – презервативы делают секс более безопасным. ■ 艾滋病是现实。在你教她生命知识时，铭记当今最重要的一条：安全套使性爱更安全。

■ الأيدز حقيقة. وعندما تعلمينها حقائق الحياة ذكريها بأهمها اليوم. إن استعمال العازل يجعل ممارسة الجنس أكثر مأمونية.

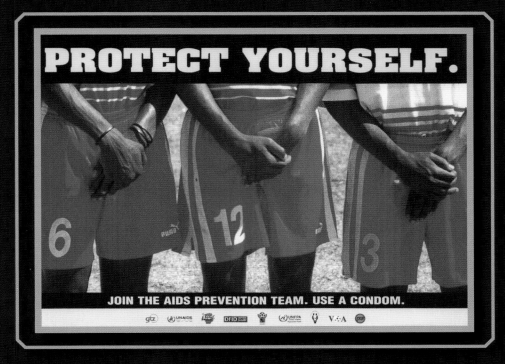

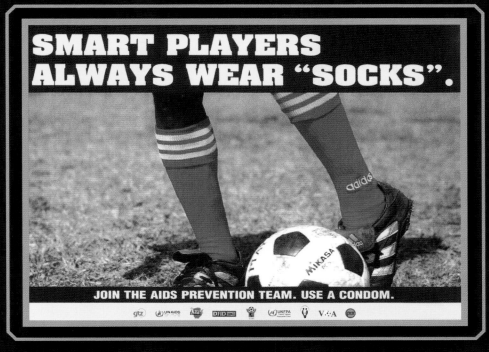

■ Protège-toi. Adhère à l'équipe de prévention du sida. Utilise un préservatif.
■ Protéjase. Únase al equipo de prevención del sida. Utilice preservativos.
■ Защити себя. Присоединись к тем, кто предупреждает СПИД. Используй презерватив. ■ 保护你自己。加入到艾滋病预防队伍中来。请使用安全套。

■ عليكم بحماية أنفسكم. انضموا إلى فريق الوقاية من الأيدز. استعملوا العازل الذكري.

■ Le joueur intelligent se protège toujours. Adhère à l'équipe de prévention du sida. Utilise un préservatif. ■ Un jugador inteligente nunca sale al campo sin protección. Únase al equipo de prevención del sida. Utilice preservativos.
■ Хорошие игроки всегда надевают защитную одежду. Присоединись к тем, кто предупреждает СПИД. Используй презерватив. ■ 精明的球员总穿着"袜子"。加入到艾滋病预防队伍中来。使用安全套。

■ اللاعبون البارعون يلبسون «الجوارب» دائماً. انضموا إلى فريق الوقاية من الأيدز. استعملوا العازل الذكري.

■ Pas d'action sans protection. ■ Sin protección, no hay acción. ■ Никаких действий без защиты. ■ 没有保护，就不要行动。
■ لا تمارس الجنس دون حماية.

■ Pas d'action sans protection. ■ Sin protección, no hay acción. ■ Никаких действий без защиты. ■ 没有保护，就不要行动。
■ لا تمارس الجنس دون حماية.

81

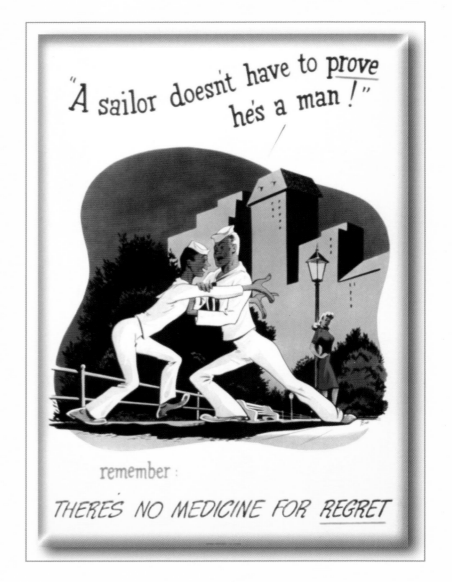

■ Go to the doctor's for a check-up. ■ Va voir le médecin.
■ Vaya al médico para una revisión. 请找医生查体。
■ عليك بمراجعة الطبيب ليفحصك.

■ Un matelot n'a pas besoin de prouver qu'il est un homme.
■ Un marinero no tiene por qué demostrar su hombría.
■ Моряку нет необходимости доказывать, что он мужчина. ■ 水手不必这样逞能。

■ البحّار ليس في حاجة إلى إثبات فحولته.

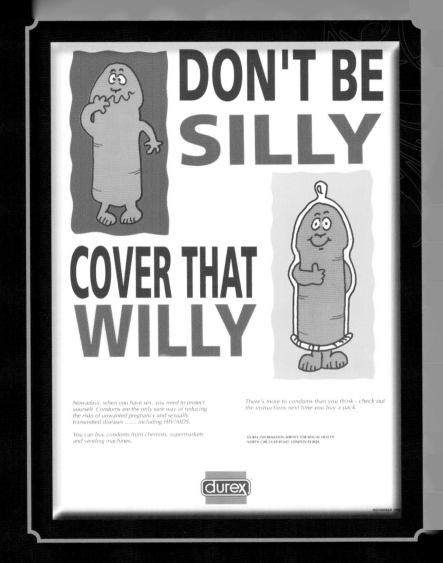

Si tu as eu deux partenaires sexuels et tes partenaires en ont eu deux …
Si has tenido dos parejas sexuales, y cada una ha tenido dos …
Если у вас два половых партнера и каждый ваш партнер имеет по
два половых партнера, каждый из которых имеет по два половых
□ партнера… ■ 如果你有了两个性伴侣，每个性伴侣曾经有两个……

■ Ne faites pas l'idiot : sortez couvert. ■ No seas cabezón, utiliza el
condón. ■ Не будь глупцом, защити молодца. ■ 可不要犯傻：
要给阳具套套。

■ لا تكن ساذجاً واستعمل العازل الذكري.

AIDS. Sharing need[l

NACAIDS

■ Partager une seringue est le meilleur moyen de transmettre le sida. ■ Compartir jeringuillas es dar carta blanca al sida.
■ СПИДу только того и надо, чтобы вы использовали одну иглу. ■ 艾滋病：共用针具就是自找麻烦。

■ الأيدز: تبادل الإبر ليس إلا طلباً للإصابة به.

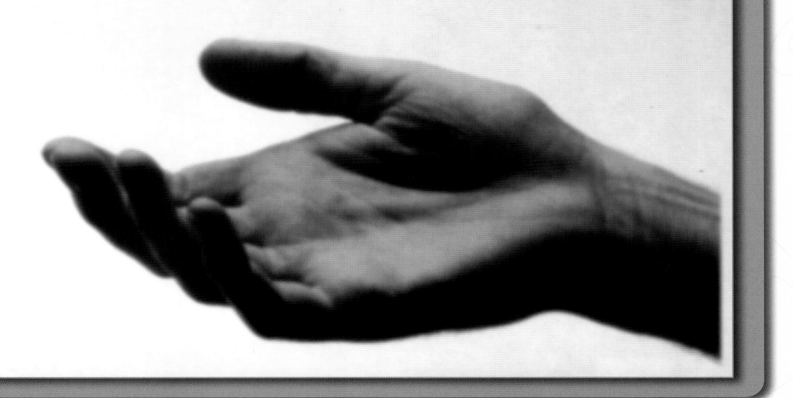

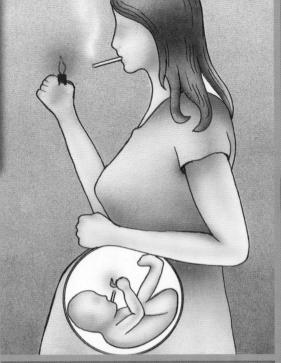

不要去做

Abstenerse

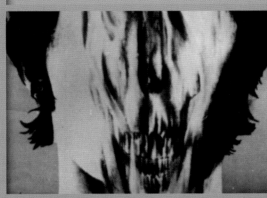

Don't

امتنعوا عن هذا

S'abstenir

Don't. From billows of cigarette smoke taking ghoulish forms to the alcohol-filled glass taking on the shape of pregnant woman's belly, public health campaigns waged against tobacco, alcohol and illicit drugs strike a familiar chord in today's society. It is surely a sign of modest success. Not long ago, the art used against tobacco and alcohol addiction was no match for the deluge of industry advertising. Equal-time requirements in the United States of America helped to push these ads off billboards and television screens, and elsewhere advertising restrictions have begun to level the playing field as well.

Still, the brand of the Marlboro Man and the logo of Benson & Hedges cut a more indelible impression than our public health images. The once high recognition level of Joe Camel among American school children, or of Peter Stuyvesant cigarettes among children in South African townships, suggests just how globalized these corporate brands have become. In contrast, the promotion of illicit drug use fills few magazine pages or television spots, but relies on peer-to-peer promotion. Ironically, as advertising restrictions on tobacco and alcohol make some markets go dark, the industries behind them have looked to creating a buzz by viral marketing on Internet. Responding to this challenge, public health campaigners have taken a page from their adversaries – creating a brand called "Truth", which has also leapt onto the Internet providing information about the tobacco industry and changing the milieu where these images duel for attention.

Inside the poster frame, public health looks for the teachable moments targeting youth, pregnant mothers, drinking and driving, and sports. Outside the poster frame, smoke-free spaces and places, age limits on drinking, and criminalization of drug possession, place these messages in a different context. How sticky is the message? Does the wilted cigarette convey a message of impotence, or is it itself impotent? It is the frame outside the frame that also matters.

But to whom does the message stick? Taxes on tobacco reduce use among current smokers, help some to quit, and stop others from starting the habit. Disproportionately, the impact of tobacco is seen among the poor and the young – often the targets of industry advertising. Too often, the education campaigns countering promotion reach the well educated, but leave behind some of the most vulnerable.

Reframing the message, campaign posters have sought to reset norms from the smooch and smell of a smoker's kiss to the idea of a designated non-drinking driver. Reframing the medium, the still image of a skeletal hand reaching out in friendship gives way to the moving image of two beer mugs colliding in an accident involving two trucks. In an age of musical remix and mash-ups, perhaps persuading youth ought to give way more often to engaging them in devising these messages.

S'abstenir. Des volutes de fumée de cigarette prenant des formes macabres au verre d'alcool rappelant le profil d'une femme enceinte, les campagnes de santé publique dirigées contre le tabac, l'alcool et la drogue sont monnaie courante aujourd'hui. C'est sûrement le signe d'un certain succès. Il n'y a pas si longtemps, l'affiche artistique utilisée dans la lutte contre le tabac et l'alcool ne pouvait pas lutter contre la déferlante publicitaire de l'industrie. Les exigences concernant l'égalité du temps de diffusion aux Etats-Unis d'Amérique ont contribué à réduire le nombre des annonces publicitaires sur affiches ou à la télévision; par ailleurs, les restrictions sur la publicité ont commencé à mettre les deux camps sur un pied d'égalité.

Le cow-boy de Marlboro et le logo de Benson & Hedges laissent toutefois une impression indélébile, ce qui n'est pas le cas de nos messages de santé publique. La renommée dont jouissait jadis Camel auprès des écoliers américains ou les cigarettes Stuyvesant chez les enfants des townships sud-africains illustre bien la mondialisation de ces marques. Par contre, on ne voit pas de publicité pour les drogues illicites dans les pages des revues ni de spots télévisés, la promotion se faisant de bouche à oreille. Paradoxalement, à la suite des restrictions sur la publicité en faveur du tabac et de l'alcool, ces industries ont cherché à utiliser le marketing viral sur Internet. Relevant le défi, les campagnes en faveur de la santé publique se sont inspirées des méthodes de leurs adversaires en créant une marque appelée « Vérité » qui s'est imposée sur Internet, fournit des informations sur l'industrie du tabac et modifie le milieu dans lequel les images se mesurent pour attirer l'attention.

Par l'affiche, la santé publique cherche à faire passer un message didactique aux jeunes, à la femme enceinte, ou concernant l'alcool au volant et le sport. Au-delà, les lieux et les espaces sans tabac, l'âge minimal fixé pour la consommation d'alcool et la criminalisation de la possession de drogues placent ces messages dans un contexte différent. Le message subsiste-t-il ? La cigarette fanée communique-t-elle un message d'impuissance ou est-ce le message lui-même qui est impuissant ? Il faut aussi tenir compte de ce qui se passe au-delà de l'affiche.

Mais chez qui le message subsiste-t-il ? Les taxes sur le tabac réduisent la consommation des fumeurs actuels, aident certains à s'arrêter de fumer et en empêchent d'autres de commencer. Les effets du tabac se font sentir de façon disproportionnée chez les pauvres et les jeunes, souvent la cible de la publicité. Trop souvent, les campagnes d'éducation destinées à contrer la promotion touchent les plus instruits mais ne parviennent pas jusqu'aux plus vulnérables.

En modifiant le message, on recherche de nouvelles normes : le baiser est lié aux relents de tabac ; un groupe d'amis confie le volant à celui qui n'a pas bu. En modifiant l'image, on recherche aussi la nouveauté : le plan fixe d'une main de squelette tendue en signe d'amitié laisse la place à l'image de deux chopes de bière se heurtant lors d'un accident de camions. Au lieu de chercher à persuader les jeunes, peut-être faudrait-il les associer davantage à la création des messages publicitaires.

Abstenerse. Presentando volutas de humo de cigarrillos que adoptan formas macabras o copas de bebidas alcohólicas que se transforman en siluetas del vientre de una embarazada, las campañas de salud pública lanzadas contra el tabaco, el alcohol y las drogas ilícitas intentan tocar la fibra sensible en la sociedad actual, en lo que supone ya una táctica corriente que revela sin duda un modesto éxito. Hasta hace poco, las imágenes empleadas contra la adicción al tabaco y el alcohol estaban muy lejos de poder contrarrestar el diluvio de publicidad de la industria. Sin embargo, la decisión de conceder el mismo tiempo a unos y a otros en los Estados Unidos de América desplazó a esos anuncios de las vallas publicitarias y las pantallas de televisión, y en otros ámbitos las restricciones a la publicidad han empezado a nivelar también el terreno de juego.

Así y todo, el hombre de Marlboro y el logotipo de Benson & Hedges causan una impresión más indeleble que nuestras imágenes de salud pública. El en otro tiempo alto nivel de reconocimiento de Joe Camel entre los escolares norteamericanos, o de los cigarrillos de Peter Stuyvesant entre los niños sudafricanos, muestra hasta qué punto se han globalizado esas marcas comerciales. En cambio, los mensajes disuasorios contra el uso de drogas ilícitas no son frecuentes en las páginas de las revistas o los anuncios televisivos, y dependen más de los consejos entre compañeros. Paradójicamente, como las restricciones a la publicidad del tabaco y el alcohol obligan a algunos de esos mercados a sumergirse, las industrias afectadas recurren a la comercialización viral a través de Internet. En respuesta a ese desafío, los defensores de la salud pública han aprendido de la experiencia de sus adversarios, creando una marca llamada «Truth» (Verdad) que también ha saltado a Internet, donde suministra información sobre la industria tabacalera. Las imágenes compiten así en un nuevo medio para captar la atención del público.

Dentro del marco del cartel, la salud pública intenta reproducir situaciones didácticas centradas en los jóvenes, las embarazadas, el alcohol y la conducción, y los deportes. Fuera del marco del cartel, los espacios y lugares sin humo, la fijación de una edad mínima para el alcohol y la penalización de la tenencia de drogas sitúan esos mensajes en un contexto diferente. ¿Tiene gancho el mensaje? ¿Transmite el cigarrillo mustio un mensaje de impotencia, o es en sí mismo un mensaje impotente? El marco que rodea al marco también es importante.

¿Para quiénes tiene gancho el mensaje? Los impuestos sobre el tabaco reducen el uso entre quienes ya fuman, ayudan a algunos a abandonar el hábito e impiden que otros empiecen a fumar. El impacto del tabaco se manifiesta desproporcionadamente entre los pobres y los jóvenes, destinatarios frecuentes de la publicidad de la industria. Demasiado a menudo, las campañas educativas emprendidas contra la promoción del tabaco llegan a los sectores más instruidos de la sociedad, pero no así a algunos de los más vulnerables.

Reformulando el mensaje, los carteles de las campañas han tomado un nuevo rumbo, pasando de intentar transmitir el mal aliento en el beso de un fumador a presentar a un conductor designado de antemano que no bebe alcohol. Reformulando el medio, la imagen estática de la mano de un esqueleto tendida para entablar amistad da paso a la imagen dinámica de dos jarras de cerveza que al toparse para brindar se transforman en dos camiones que colisionan. En una era de mezclas y remezclas musicales, tal vez habría que intentar más a menudo no tanto persuadir a los jóvenes como hacerles participar en la creación de esos mensajes.

Не делайте этого. Используя изображения от волн табачного дыма, приобретающих самые мерзкие формы, до наполненного алкоголем бокала в виде живота беременной женщины, кампании общественного здравоохранения, направленные против табака, алкоголя и наркомании, задевают знакомые струны в современном обществе. Несомненно, это является признаком довольно скромного успеха. Не так давно изобразительные средства, используемые против табачной и алкогольной зависимости не шли ни в какое сравнение с огромным потоком промышленной рекламы. Принятые в Соединенных Штатах Америки требования равного рекламного времени помогли убрать эту рекламу с рекламных щитов и экранов телевизоров, и повсюду ограничения на рекламу также начали выравнивать шансы для обеих сторон.

До сих пор торговая марка "человека из страны Мальборо" и фирменный знак "Бенсон энд Хедж" оставляют более длительное впечатление, чем наши изображения общественного здравоохранения. Однажды достигнутый высокий уровень признания Джо Кэмэла среди американских школьников или сигарет "Питер Стьюзанд" детьми в южноафриканских поселения как раз и свидетельствует о том, насколько глобализованными стали эти корпоративные фирменные наименования. В отличие от этого, пропаганда против незаконного употребления наркотиков заполняет лишь немногие страницы газет и журналов или телевизионной рекламы и основывается на принципе пропаганды среди сверстников. Однако, по мере того, как ограничения на табак и алкоголь сокращают некоторые рынки, эти отрасли промышленности пытаются использовать принципы «вирусного маркетинга» в сети Интернет. Отвечая на этот вызов, лица, занимающиеся кампаниями в области общественного здравоохранения, частично заимствовали методы у своих противников и создали под фирменным наименованием "Достоверные факты" страницу, которая также была размещена в Интернете и давала информацию о табачной промышленности и изменяла среду, в которой эти изображения стремились обратить на себя внимание.

На самом плакате общественное здравоохранение стремится изобразить поучительные моменты, акцентируя внимание на молодежь, беременных женщин, на вождение в состоянии опьянения и на спорт. За пределами плакатов помещения и места без табачного дыма, ограничение на возраст для употребления спиртных напитков, уголовное наказание за обладание при себе наркотиков - все это помещает эти сообщения в другой контекст. Насколько усваиваемыми (или "пристающими") являются эти сообщения? Передает ли изображение "увядшей" сигареты сообщение об импотенции или же оно само не обладает потенцией? Это те рамки, за пределами рамок плаката, которые также имеют значение.

Но к кому "пристает" сообщение? Налоги на табак сокращают употребление среди нынешних курильщиков, помогают некоторым из них бросить курить и останавливают тех, кто хочет начать курить. Табак диспропорционально воздействует на бедных людей и молодежь, которые часто являются мишенями для рекламы табачной промышленности. Просветительские кампании контррекламы чаще всего достигают более образованных людей, но не достигают некоторых из самых уязвимых.

Изменяя сообщение, используемые в кампании плакаты направлены на смену норм от вкуса и запаха поцелуя курильщика до идеи настоящего непьющего водителя. Изменяя носитель сообщения, застывшее изображение дружеского объятья руки скелета уступает место движущемуся изображению двух бокалов пива, сталкивающихся в аварии двух грузовиков. В наше время музыкальных ремиксов и смешивания мелодий методы убеждения молодых людей, вероятно, должны уступить более частому привлечению их к созданию таких средств воздействия.

■ 不要去做。 从恐怖形式的滚滚烟雾，到形似孕妇肚子的盛酒杯子，反对吸烟、饮酒和使用非法药物的公共卫生宣传活动拨动了当今社会一个熟悉的心弦。这确实象征着一个不太大的成就。不久前，用来反对吸烟和酒精成瘾的艺术创作，与汹涌而来的工业宣传广告根本无以伦比。在美国，等同时间的要求有助于把这些广告挤出广告牌和电视荧屏。在其它地方，广告限制也已经使得游戏场变得平等。

万宝路男人（Marlboro Man）的品牌和本海孜（Benson & Hedges）的标识与我们的公共卫生图像相比，更能给人留下不可磨灭的印象。乔骆驼（Joe Camel）在美国学校儿童中，或者彼德·史蒂文森（Peter Stuyvesant）香烟在南非城镇的儿童中曾一度获得了高度认可，这表明企业品牌做到了如此的全球化。相反，非法用药的宣传仅仅占据了极少的杂志页面或电视短节目，而依靠的却是同伴宣传。令人啼笑皆非的是，在烟草和酒精的广告宣传受到限制，使得一些市场陷入暗淡之后，其背后的制造业转而利用网络病毒营销的方式来制造传闻。为了应对这种挑战，公共卫生活动家从对手那里获得一个页面，创立一个名为"真理"的品牌，同时迅速将其放在英特网上，提供烟草业的情况，并更改这些图像能够引起关注的背景。

在海报框架内，公共卫生寻找的是针对年轻人、孕妇、酒后驾车和体育运动的可教时机。在海报框架外，寻找无烟空间和地点、饮酒年龄限制，以及药品持有犯罪，并把这些主题内容置于不同的背景下加以考虑。这些主题内容难缠吗？枯萎的香烟是否表达了阳痿的信息？或它不起作用？框架之外的框架也是要紧的。

但是，这些主题内容对谁来说难缠呢？征收烟草税可减少现有吸烟者的吸烟量，有助于一些人戒烟，阻止一些人染上吸烟习惯。烟草对穷人和年轻人产生的影响特别大，他们常常是烟草业广告宣传的对象。与反促销相对应的宣教活动通常触及受过良好教育的人们，把一些最脆弱的人员抛在了后面。

为了主题内容的重新构思，活动海报从吸烟者亲吻的污迹和气味到特定不饮酒司机的猜想，力求重新确立规范。为了宣传工具的重新构思，一只骨瘦如柴的手伸出去寻找友谊这样的静止图像，应该向两个啤酒杯在两个卡车事故中相碰的移动图像做出让步。在音乐混合和杂乱的时代，劝说年轻人的做法应该时常向年轻人参与设计主题内容的做法做出让步。

 امتنعوا عن هذا. من سُحب دخان السجائر التي تتخذ أشكالاً مروعة إلى الأكواب المملوءة بالكحول التي تتخذ شكل بطن المرأة الحامل شنت حملات الصحة العمومية هجومها على التبغ والكحول وعزفت على وتر حساس في المجتمعات اليوم. ويُعد هذا بالطبع دليلاً على تواضع النجاح الذي تحقق. ومنذ فترة ليست بالطويلة لم تكن الأعمال الفنية المستخدمة في مكافحة التبغ وإدمان الكحول تجاري طوفان الإعلانات التي تقوم بها دوائر الصناعة. وتطلب الأمر وقتاً مماثلاً في الولايات المتحدة الأمريكية للمساعدة على إقصاء هذه الإعلانات عن لوحات الإعلانات وشاشات التليفزيون، وبدأ في أماكن أخرى فرض قيود على الإعلان كي تكون المواجهة على قدم المساواة.

وماز الت العلامة التجارية الممثلة في الرجل الذي يدخن سيجارة من نوع مارلبورو، وشعار شركة Benson & Hedges يعطيان انطباعاً يصعب محوه مقارنة بالصور التي نستعملها في ملصقات الصحة العمومية. ويدل تحديداً مستوى التقدير المرتفع الذي بلغته يوماً شركة «جو كامل» بين أطفال المدارس أو سجائر شركة «بيتر ستيوفيزانت» بين أطفال بلدات جنوب أفريقيا على مدى الانتشار العالمي للعلامتين التجاريتين لهاتين الشركتين. وعلى النقيض من ذلك فإن الترويج للعقاقير غير المشروعة لا يملأ إلا القليل من صفحات المجلات أو إعلانات التليفزيون، ولكنه يعتمد على الترويج لها بين الأفراد. ومما يبعث على السخرية أنه نظراً لأن القيود المفروضة على الإعلان عن التبغ والكحول تصيب بعض الأسواق بالكساد، أن هذه الصناعة من ورائها عملت على إشاعة التسويق المحموم بين الناس على شبكة الانترنت. ولمواجهة هذا التحدي التقط أصحاب حملات الصحة العمومية الخيط من خصومهم، واستحدثوا علامة تجارية تسمى «الحقيقة» ثم نشروها أيضا على شبكة الانترنت وهي توفر معلومات عن دوائر صناعة التبغ وتغير الساحة التي تتنافس فيها هاتان الصورتان على استرعاء الانتباه.

وداخل إطار الملصق الإعلاني تبحث دوائر الصحة العمومية عن لحظات ملائمة للتعليم تستهدف فيها الشباب والحوامل ومواضيع مثل الشرب والقيادة والألعاب الرياضية. وخارج إطار الملصق الإعلاني توضع الرسائل الخاصة بالمساحات والأماكن الخالية من دخان التبغ والحدود السنية للشرب وتجريم حيازة المخدرات في سياقات مختلفة. ولكن ما مدى رسوخ الرسالة؟ هل تنقل السجائر المطفأة رسالة عن العجز أم أن الرسالة هي نفسها عاجزة؟ إنه الإطار الخارج عن الإطار هو الذي يهم دائماً.

ولكن بمن تعلق الرسالة؟ إن الضرائب المفروضة على التبغ تقلل تعاطيه بين المدخنين الحاليين، وتساعد البعض على الإقلاع عنه، وتجعل الآخرين يحجمون عن البدء في هذه العادة. ويمكن رؤية الأثر غير المتناسب للتبغ بين الفقراء والشباب، وهما الفئتان المستهدفتان غالباً بإعلانات دوائر صناعة التبغ. وفي أغلب الأحيان تصل حملات التوعية بالدعاية المضادة إلى المتعلمين ولكنها تخلف وراءها بعضاً من أسرع الفئات تأثراً.

وكان الغرض من إعادة صياغة أسلوب الرسائل والملصقات الإعلانية للحملات هو إعادة وضع القواعد التي تنبني عليها، من ملمس قُبلة المدخن ورائحة قبلته إلى فكرة قائد السيارة الذي لا يشرب الكحول. وبإعادة صياغة وسيلة نقل الرسالة تترك الصورة الجامدة ليد الهيكل العظمي الممدودة لمصافحة صديق مكانها للصورة المتحركة لكأسين من البيرة يرتطمان ببعضهما في حادث سيارة. وفي عصر يتم فيه إعادة توزيع التسجيلات الموسيقية وتقديمها في ثوب جديد قد يتعين إقناع الشباب أكثر فأكثر من خلال إشراكهم في نقل هذه الرسائل.

أنتوني د. صو، برنامج الصحة العالمية وإتاحة التكنولوجيا، معهد تيري سانفورد للسياسات العمومية، جامعة ديوك، دورام، نورث كارولينا، الولايات المتحدة الأمريكية.

■ The snake and the cigarette: both are enemies of the people. Keep away from them. ■ Le serpent et la cigarette: deux ennemis publics. Evitons-les! ■ La serpiente y el cigarrillo: dos enemigos públicos. Pon terreno por medio ■ Змея и сигареты - враги человека. Держитесь от них подальше. ■ 毒蛇与卷烟：均为人类之敌。请远离它们。

■ الثعبان والسيجارة عدوان للناس فابتعد عنهما.

■ Travail sans tabac : franchissons le pas – Journée mondiale sans tabac, 31 mai 1992. ■ Lugares de trabajo sin humo de tabaco: más seguros y más sanos – lema del Día Mundial Sin Tabaco, 31 de mayo de 1992. ■ Бездымная среда на рабочем месте - более безопасная и более здоровая среда! Всемирный день без табака, 31 мая 1992 г. ■ 工作场所不吸烟：更安全、更健康：1992年5月31日世界无烟日。

■ أماكن العمل الخالية من التبغ أماكن عمل أسلم وأصح: اليوم العالمي للامتناع عن التدخين، 31 أيار/ مايو 1992.

Hei gët nët gefëmmt!

Frësch Loft
fir eng Generatioun
ouni Tubak

MINISTERE DE LA SANTE
LUXEMBOURG

MOTIVÉ ?

La liberté au bout du fil

pour vous aider à arrêter
TABAC-STOP
☎ 45 30 33
tous les mardis

FONDATION LUXEMBOURGEOISE
CONTRE LE CANCER

○ smoking here! Fresh air for a tobacco-free generation. ■ Ici, on ne ⬚ pas! De l'air pur pour une génération sans tabac. ■ Prohibido fumar. ⬚ puro para una generación sin tabaco. ■ Здесь курить запрещается! ⬚ый воздух для поколения без дыма. ■ 此处禁止吸烟。为了无烟世 ⬚ 保持空气清新。

■ Are you motivated? Ring this number if you are. ■ ¿Motivado? L⬚ libertad está al otro lado del teléfono. ■ Решились? Позвони по эт⬚ номеру. ■ 你有决心吗？随时打电话。

ل لديك الحافز. اتصل بهذا الرقم؟

■ Smoking gun. ■ La fumée est mortelle. ■ Cada cigarillo es una bala. ■ Сигарета убивает! ■ 每一支烟就像是一粒子弹。

■ السيجارة تقضي عليك.

■ Public places and transport: don't smoke, don't smoke us out. May 31st World tobacco-free day. ■ Transporte y espacios publicos. No fume, no ah demás. 31 de mayo de 1991 – Día Mundial Sin Tabaco. ■ Общественные транспорт. Не курите сами и нас не окуривайте. 31 мая 1991 г. Всемир без табака. ■ 在公共场所和交通工具上请不要吸烟，不要把我们熏跑。31日世界无烟日。

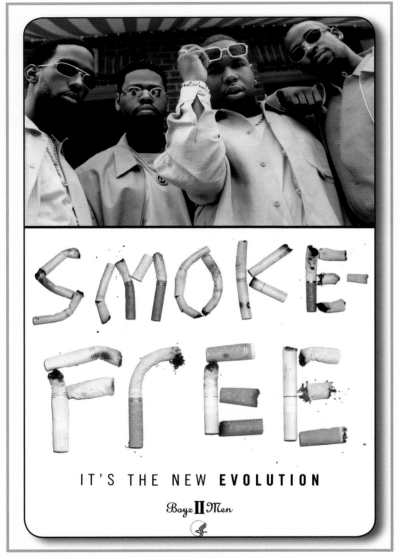

■ Sans tabac: c'est l'évolution nouvelle. ■ Sin humo: la nueva evolución. ■ Без дыма - это современно. ■ 不吸烟：这是新发展。

■ الخلو من دخان التبغ: إنها ثورة جديدة.

■ Mannequin depuis 14 ans ; c'est la photo de moi que je préfère. ■ Catorce años trabajando de modelo... y ésta es mi foto preferida. ■ Я являюсь моделью уже 14 лет, и я люблю эту фотографию. ■ 当了14年模特，这是我自己最喜欢的一张拍片。

■ أعتبر هذه لقطتي المفضلة خلال 14 عاماً عملت فيها عارضة أزياء.

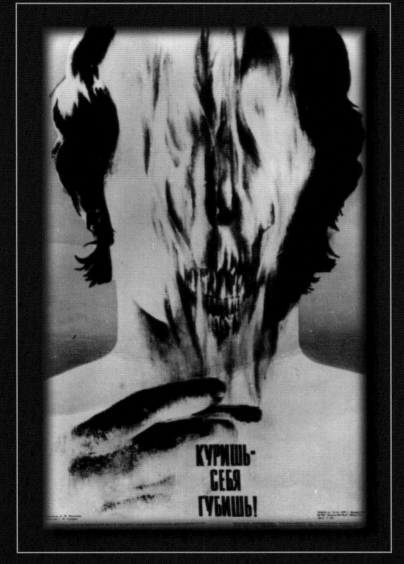

■ Améliore ta performance : sport et tabac ne font pas bon ménage ! ■ Mejora tu juego: deporte y tabaco no son buenos amigos. ■ Играй лучше! Спорт и табак несовместимы! ■ 提高你的比赛成绩：体育与烟草不相容！

■ حسنوا لعبتكم: الرياضة والتبغ لا يجتمعان!

■ Smoke and die. ■ Tu fumes, tu meurs. ■ Quien fuma se autodestruye. ■ 吸烟与死亡。

■ دخن لتدمر نفسك.

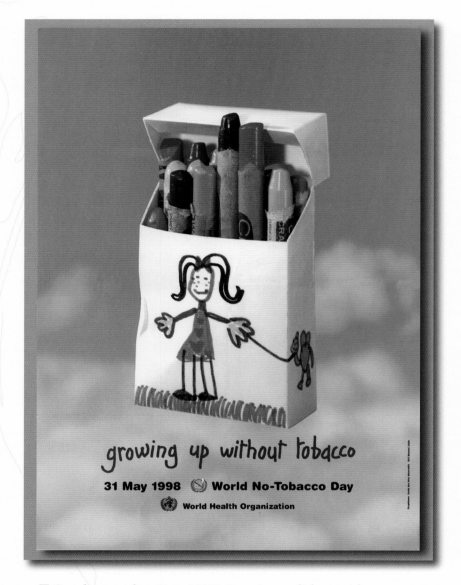

growing up without tobacco

31 May 1998 🚭 **World No-Tobacco Day**
World Health Organization

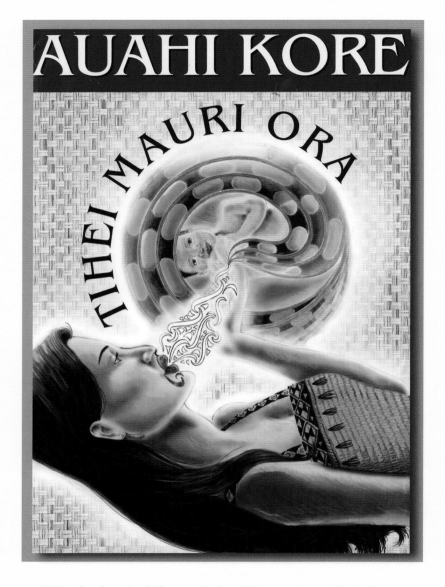

AUAHI KORE

TIHEI MAURI ORA

■ Grandir sans tabac, 31 mai 1998, Journée mondiale sans tabac.
■ Crecer sin tabaco – lema del Día Mundial Sin Tabaco, 31 de mayo de 1998. ■ Растем без табака. 31 мая 1998 г. Всемирный день без табака.
■ 在无烟环境中成长。1998年5月31日世界无烟日。
■ حتى يكبر الأطفال دون أن يستعبدهم التبغ، 31 أيار / مايو 1998، اليوم العالمي للامتناع عن التدخين.

■ The first breath of life – smoke free. ■ Le premier souffle de la vie: sans tabac. ■ El primer aliento de vida. Libre de tabaco. ■ Первый глоток воздуха - без дыма. ■ 生命的第一口气——没有烟雾。
■ حتى لا يتأثر الجنين - التحرر من دخان التبغ.

96

■ Mum, is that a way to treat your baby? ■ Maman, c'est comme ça que tu traites ton enfant ? ■ ¡Mamá! ¿así tratas a tu hijo? ■ Мама, разве это нужно твоему ребенку? ■ 母亲，你愿意婴儿这样做吗？

■ Alcohol and tobacco take the bloom from your beauty. ■ El alcohol y el tabaco acaban marchitando la belleza. ■ Алкоголь и табак отнимают у вас красоту. ■ 酒精和烟草令你的美貌失色。

■ الكحول والتبغ يجعلان جمالك يذوي ويذبل.

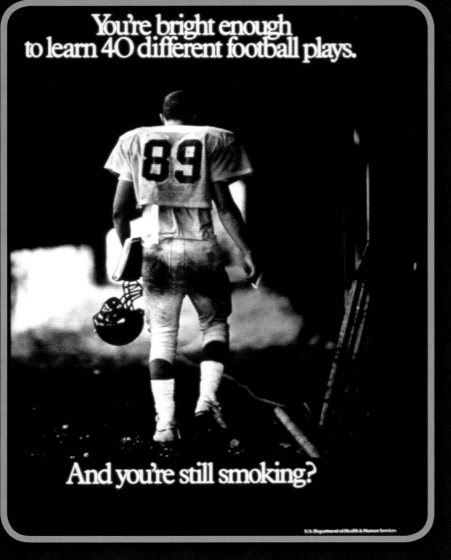

You're bright enough
to learn 40 different football plays.

89

And you're still smoking?

U.S. Department of Health & Human Services

You have enough smarts to rebuild an engine.

And you're still smoking?

■ Tu es assez intelligent pour reconstruire un moteur … et tu fumes encore ?
■ Eres suficientemente listo para reconstruir un motor … ¿y sigues fumando?
■ Вы достаточно умелы, чтобы отремонтировать двигатель. И продолжаете курить? ■ 你的聪明才智足以再造引擎。可你还在吸烟吗?
■ أتكون لديك البراعة الكافية لتجديد محرك وتستمر في التدخين؟

■ Tu es assez intelligent pour apprendre 40 combinaisons différentes … et tu fumes encore ? ■ Eres suficientemente listo para aprenderte 40 estrategias de juego diferentes … ¿y sigues fumando? ■ Вы достаточно умны, чтобы выучить 40 различных спортивных игр. И продолжаете курить? ■ 你很聪明，能够学会足球比赛40多种不同打法。可你还在吸烟吗?
■ أيكون لديك الذكاء الكافي لفهم 40 حركة مختلفة من حركات كرة القدم وتستمر في التدخين؟

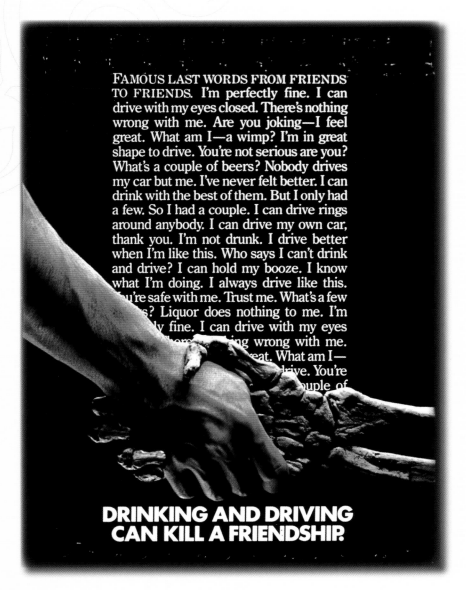

FAMOUS LAST WORDS FROM FRIENDS TO FRIENDS. I'm perfectly fine. I can drive with my eyes closed. There's nothing wrong with me. Are you joking—I feel great. What am I—a wimp? I'm in great shape to drive. You're not serious are you? What's a couple of beers? Nobody drives my car but me. I've never felt better. I can drink with the best of them. But I only had a few. So I had a couple. I can drive rings around anybody. I can drive my own car, thank you. I'm not drunk. I drive better when I'm like this. Who says I can't drink and drive? I can hold my booze. I know what I'm doing. I always drive like this. You're safe with me. Trust me. What's a few ...s? Liquor does nothing to me. I'm ...ly fine. I can drive with my eyes ... wrong with me. ...reat. What am I— ...drive. You're ...uple of

DRINKING AND DRIVING CAN KILL A FRIENDSHIP.

■ L'alcool au volant peut tuer une amitié. ■ Ponerse al volante después de haber consumido alcohol puede ser el final de una amistad. ■ Пьяный за рулем может убить друга. ■ 酒后驾车殃及友情。

■ شرب الكحول والقيادة يمكن أن يقضيا على الصداقة.

■ This is a crime. ■ C'est un crime. ■ Esto es un crimen. ■ 这可是犯罪。
■ إنها جريمة.

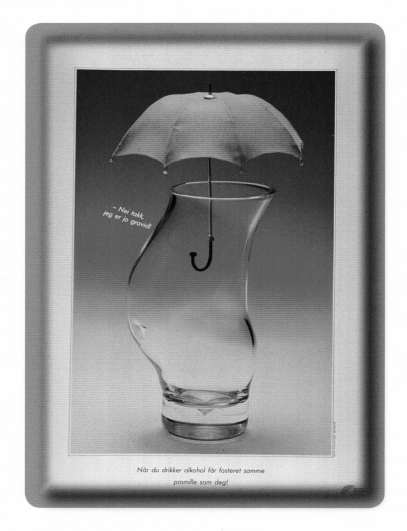

No thanks, I'm pregnant. ■ Non merci, je suis enceinte.
■ No gracias, estoy embarazada. ■ Нет, спасибо, я беременна. ■ 不，谢谢。我已有身孕。
لا، شكراً جزيلاً فأنا حامل. ■

Daddy, please don't drink. ■ Papa, je t'en prie, ne bois pas.
■ Papá, por favor no bebas. ■ 爸爸，请不要喝酒。
أبي لا تشرب الكحول أرجوك. ■

L'entretien des alcooliques et de leurs victimes coûte <u>chaque année</u> à l'assistance publique suisse, donc aux con=tribuables, *20 millions de francs.* Cette somme <u>dépensée chaque année</u> représente la valeur d'un troupeau de *25 mille* têtes de gros bétail.

NON ECCEDERE NEL CONSUMO DI ALCOLICI

■ Don't drink too much alcohol.
■ Il est dangereux de boire trop d'alcool.
■ No consumas alcohol en exceso.
■ Не злоупотребляй алкоголем.
■ 不要过度饮酒。
■ لا تفرط في استهلاك الكحول.

■ Each year looking after alcoholics costs the Swiss welfare services – that means the taxpayer – 20 million francs (the value of 25 thousand head of cattle). ■ La atención a los alcohólicos impone cada año a la salud pública suiza – y, por ende, a los contribuyentes – un gasto de 20 millones de francos (valor que equivale a 25 000 cabezas de ganado). ■ Оказание помощи больным алкоголизмом и их жертвам обходится ежегодно службам соцобеспечения Швейцарии и, следовательно, налогоплательщикам в 20 миллионов франков (что сравнимо стоимости 25 тысяч голов скота). ■ 瑞士福利局（即纳税人）花费2000万瑞郎（价值相当于2.5万头牛）照管嗜酒者。

■ اجتماع مدمني الكحول وضحاياهم يكلف إدارة الإعانات العمومية في سويسرا، ومن ثم يكلف دافعي الضرائب، 20 مليون فرنك سنوياً.

■ A la mode/passé de mode.
■ En la onda / fuera de onda.
■ Начало / Конец. ■ 流行的/过时的。

■ دخول/ خروج.

■ Le sevré fait un tabac! ■ Todos te querrán si lo dejas.
■ Все любят тех, кто смог бросить курить. ■ 戒烟者受欢迎。

■ الكل يحب من ينجح في الامتناع عن التدخين.

■ Certains parents boivent trop … et ça fait mal. Si tu veux en savoir plus, adresse-toi à quelqu'un en qui tu as confiance. ■ Algunos padres y madres toman demasiado alcohol, y no es fácil convivir con eso. Si quieres más información, dirígete a alguien de confianza. ■ Некоторые родители пьют слишком много - это причиняет боль. Хочешь узнать больше - спроси того, кому ты доверяешь. ■ 有些爸爸妈妈饮酒过多—这会带来危害。 如欲了解更多情况，请向你信任的人询问。

■ بعض الأمهات والآباء يفرط في شرب الكحول وهذا الأمر يؤذيهم. إذا كنت تريد معرفة المزيد اسأل أحد من تثق فيه.

SIDA /MOH REPRODUCTIVE HEALTH PROJECT 1996/1997

MINISTRY OF HEALTH
(Division of Family Health)

■ Ne buvez pas de l'alcool frelaté. C'est risqué. ■ No bebas chang'aa: Si caes dentro, te resultará difícil salir. ■ Не пей самогон. Выбраться будет трудно! ■ 不要喝烈性自酿酒：这会难以自拔。

■ لا تتناول هذا الشراب: ستدخل في محنة يصعب الخروج منها.

■ With alcohol you'll discover new sensations. ■ L'alcool te fera découvrir des sensations nouvelles. ■ Это те новые ощущения, которые тебе даст алкоголь. ■ 用了酒精，你会发现感觉异常。

■ الكحول يجعلك تكتشفين أحاسيس جديدة.

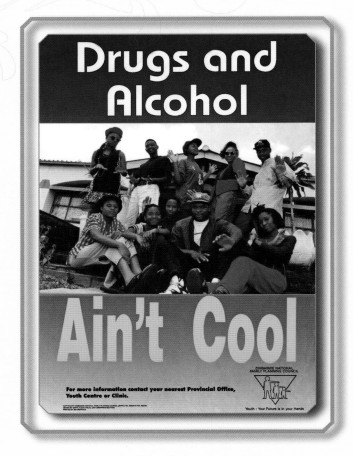

■ Les drogues et l'alcool, c'est pas cool. ■ Drogas y alcohol: mala onda. ■ Наркотики и алкоголь - вовсе не так здорово. ■ 吸毒和饮酒，根本不酷。

■ المخدرات والكحول ليسا بالأمر الجيد.

■ Drug addiction is suicide. ■ Toxicomanie = suicide. ■ Drogas = suicidio. ■ 吸毒成瘾就是自杀。

■ إدمان المخدرات انتحار.

Cocaína. Hay trenes que es mejor NO coger

www.pnsd.msc.es

Estar irritable, comer mal, dormir poco, tener paranoias o alucinaciones, sufrir taquicardias, perder el control, mayor accidentabilidad, problemas cardiovasculares y sexuales... Es así de fácil. Si consumes cocaína, sola o en combinación con otras drogas, éste será tu tren de vida ¿De verdad quieres subir?

MINISTERIO DE SANIDAD Y CONSUMO

pnsd

DROGASDR

■ Cocaine: there are some trains it's best not to take. ■ Cocaïne : il est des trains à bord desquels il vaut mieux ne pas monter. ■ Кокаин. Есть пути, на которые лучше не вставать. ■ 可卡因：有些火车，最好不要坐。

■ الكوكايين: هناك بعض القطارات التي من الأفضل ألا نركبها.

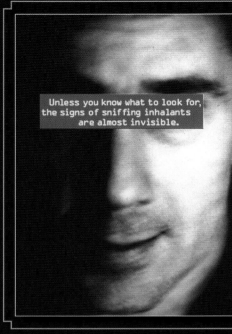

Unless you know what to look for, the signs of sniffing inhalants are almost invisible.

If your child has paint stains on his fingers and mouth, excessive vomiting and watery eyes, he may be inhaling the fumes from products like spray paint, nail polish and gasoline. Nearly one in four kids has abused them by seventh grade. Call 1-800-269-4237, and face this problem with both eyes open. ☆ TEXAS PREVENTION PARTNERSHIP

◼ Produits inhalés : si tu ne sais pas ce que tu cherches, les signes sont presque invisibles. ◼ Es difícil saber si alguien toma sustancias inhalables, salvo que se conozcan los efectos asociados a su consumo. ◼ Если вы не знаете о чем идет речь, признаки вдыхания вредных летучих веществ почти незаметны. ◼ 除非你知道要寻找什么，毒品溶解物的吸入表象几乎难以望见。

◼ إذا كنت لا تعرف فعلا ما تنشق المواد لا تكاد تلحظ.

◼ Nous voulons te présenter la cocaïne des années 90. Ton fils connaît peut-être déjà. ◼ Queremos presentarle la cocaína de los años noventa, que quizá le resulte ya familiar a su hijo. ◼ Мы хотели бы рассказать вам о проблеме кокаина в 1990-е годы. Ваш ребенок, возможно, уже с ним знаком. ◼ 我们向你介绍90年代的可卡因情况，你的孩子可能已经了解。

◼ نود توعيتك بشأن الكوكايين الذي شاع تعاطيه في التسعينات. قد يكون طفلك على علم بهذا فعلاً.

◼ Cette pub te dira des choses à propos des produits inhalés que ta fille te cachera. ◼ Lea este anuncio y aprenderá algunas cosas sobre el consumo de sustancias inhalables que su hija tal vez prefiera no contarle. ◼ Этот плакат расскажет вам о вдыхании летучих веществ то, о чем ваша дочь предпочитает умалчивать. ◼ 本广告是关于吸入毒品溶解物方面的信息，你的孩子可能没有告诉你。

◼ هذا الإعلان سوف يخبرك بأمرين عن نشق المواد من المستبعد أن يستسيغهما طفلك.

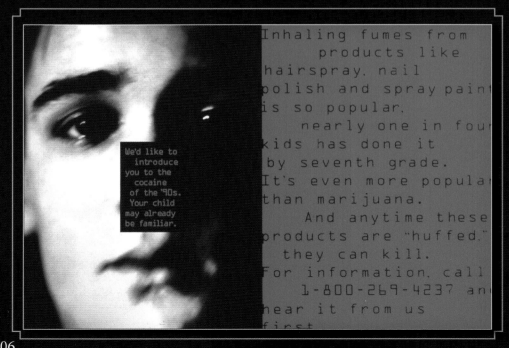

We'd like to introduce you to the cocaine of the '90s. Your child may already be familiar.

Inhaling fumes from products like hairspray, nail polish and spray paint is so popular. nearly one in four kids has done it by seventh grade. It's even more popular than marijuana. And anytime these products are "huffed," they can kill. For information, call 1-800-269-4237 and hear it from us first

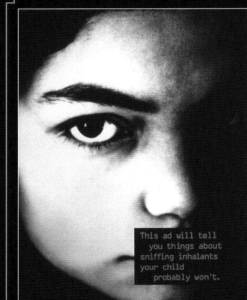

This ad will tell you things about sniffing inhalants your child probably won't.

Inhaling the fumes of products like correction fluid, nail polish and spray paint is so popular, nearly one in four kids has tried it by seventh grade. And anytime these products are "huffed," they can kill. For information, call 1-800-269-4237, or ask your child. They may know more than they are telling. ☆ TEXAS PREVENTION PARTNERSHIP

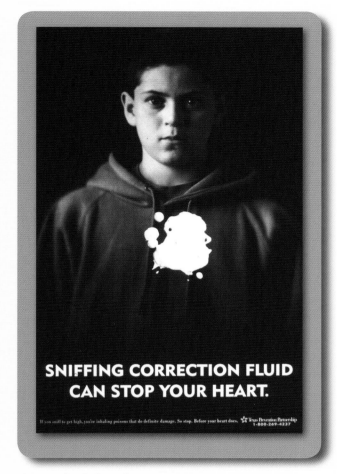

SNIFFING CORRECTION FLUID CAN STOP YOUR HEART.

If you sniff to get high, you're inhaling poisons that do definite damage. So stop. Before your heart does. ☆ Texas Prevention Partnership 1-800-269-4237

SNIFFING MARKERS DESTROYS YOUR BRAIN.

Sniffing stuff like spray paint or markers can cause brain damage, lung damage, even death. ☆ Texas Prevention Partnership 1-800-269-4237

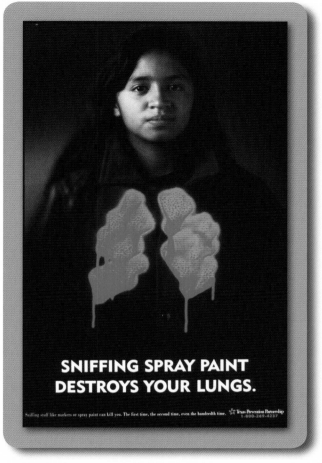

SNIFFING SPRAY PAINT DESTROYS YOUR LUNGS.

Sniffing stuff like markers or spray paint can kill you. The first time, the second time, even the hundredth time. ☆ Texas Prevention Partnership 1-800-269-4237

■ Sniffer du liquide correcteur peut provoquer un arrêt du cœur. ■ La inhalación de líquido corrector puede provocarte un paro cardíaco. ■ Вдыхание паров корректирующей жидкости может остановить ваше сердце. ■ 吸入涂改液，可使心跳停止。

■ إن نشق المواد المنبعثة من السوائل الماسحة يمكن أن يوقف قلبك عن العمل.

■ Sniffer des marqueurs détruit ton cerveau. ■ La inhalación de rotuladores puede destrozarte el cerebro. ■ Вдыхание паров маркера разрушает ваш мозг. ■ 吸入记号笔水，会损害大脑。

■ إن نشق الأقلام اللبادية يدمر دماغك.

■ Sniffer un spray de peinture détruit tes poumons. ■ La inhalación de aerosoles puede destrozarte los pulmones. ■ Вдыхание паров краски разрушает ваши легкие. ■ 吸入喷雾油漆，会损害你的肺脏。

■ إن نشق مواد الطلاء المرشوشة يدمر رئتيك.

107

Be safe

حافظوا على
سلامتكم

保证安全

Promouvoir
la sécurité

Обеспечьте
безопасность

Promover
la seguridad

Be safe. Comply! Avoid! Beware! Do! Do Not! Follow Procedure! When a society industrializes, sooner or later people become aware of the risks in their new environment and safety becomes a desirable goal.

Normally, safety starts in factories with the introduction of safer machines that protect the operator from dangerous parts. Then human behaviour comes into the equation: people themselves need to be encouraged to act safely. These two approaches combine naturally and over the years have been the focus of education campaigns which have led to substantial reductions in the number of accidents in the workplace. Posters have played a key role in safety propaganda, using simple messages about handling tools and operating machines safely, and generally being careful in the workplace. The posters in this chapter appeal to the personal responsibility of the worker, to physical self-preservation, comradeship and also often to responsibility to one's family.

Safety posters look very similar regardless of where they originate. Both Chinese and Indian clothes can get caught in unprotected machines, resulting in the same awful accidents seen in European or American factories. But unfortunately, the distribution of safety risks – as with that of wealth – is uneven. The number of occupational accidents is higher in developing countries where poverty and lack of legal protection conspire to push safety issues down the workplace agenda.

The safety movement is part of a larger drive to protect society at large. So it is no wonder we see comparable messages evolving on traffic safety, health and fire prevention. In the home, it is also better to be safe and there are now agencies set up to tell individual citizens how to achieve domestic safety. In many parts of the world this approach has had a positive effect on the lives of many people; but there is also a growing realization – illustrated through some of the posters – that safety issues nowadays go deeper than the simple carelessness that was the focus in the past. What danger do people seek to combat by keeping guns in their homes? What use is it to ask for protection against breathing unclean air in a factory, when pollution can be blown into your home from far away?

Promouvoir la sécurité. Respecter ! Eviter ! Attention ! Faire ! Ne pas faire ! Suivre la procédure indiquée ! Lorsqu'une société s'industrialise, tôt ou tard on prend conscience des risques dans l'environnement nouveau et la sécurité devient un but en soi.

En général, la sécurité commence dans les usines par l'introduction de machines dont certaines parties sont isolées pour ne pas présenter de danger pour l'opérateur. Puis on tient compte du comportement humain : il faut amener les gens eux-mêmes à respecter les consignes de sécurité. Ces deux approches se combinent naturellement et font depuis des années l'objet de campagnes qui ont permis d'aboutir à des réductions sensibles des accidents du travail. Les affiches ont joué un rôle essentiel dans la diffusion des messages de sécurité au moyen d'une série de textes simples, indiquant comment utiliser des outils et des machines sans courir le risque d'avoir un accident et, d'une manière générale, comment être prudent sur le lieu de travail. Les affiches de ce chapitre font appel à la responsabilité personnelle de l'ouvrier, à son instinct de conservation, à son esprit de camaraderie et souvent aussi à la responsabilité à l'égard de sa famille.

Les messages de sécurité sont très semblables dans les différentes parties du monde : en Chine et en Inde, les vêtements peuvent se prendre dans les rouages de machines qui ne sont pas protégées et causer des accidents identiques à ceux que l'on a connu dans des usines européennes ou américaines. Mais malheureusement, comme les richesses, les risques en matière de sécurité sont inégalement répartis. Le nombre des accidents du travail est plus élevé dans les pays en développement où, en raison de la pauvreté et de l'absence de protection juridique, les problèmes de sécurité ne sont pas au centre des préoccupations dans les milieux professionnels.

Le mouvement en faveur de la sécurité s'inscrit aussi dans un effort plus large visant à protéger la société dans son ensemble. On ne doit pas s'étonner de voir des messages du même type sur la sécurité routière, la protection de la santé ou la prévention des incendies. Comme il faut aussi être prudent chez soi, des organisations dont le but est de promouvoir la sécurité au foyer ont été créées. Dans de nombreuses régions du monde, cette approche a eu un effet positif sur la vie de nombreuses personnes ; mais on est aussi de plus en plus conscients – comme l'illustrent certaines des affiches – que la sécurité ne consiste plus seulement aujourd'hui à prévenir l'inattention comme avant. Contre quel danger essaie-t-on de se prémunir en gardant des armes à feu à domicile ? A quoi cela sert-il de vouloir se protéger de la pollution de l'air à l'usine si la pollution atmosphérique venue de loin vous affecte à la maison ?

Promover la seguridad. ¡Cumple esto! ¡Evita lo otro! ¡Ten cuidado! ¡Haz esto! ¡No hagas lo otro! ¡Atente a las normas! Cuando una sociedad se industrializa, tarde o temprano la gente adquiere conciencia de los riesgos presentes en su nuevo entorno y la seguridad se convierte en un objetivo a alcanzar.

El proceso comienza normalmente en las fábricas con la introducción de máquinas más seguras que protegen a los trabajadores de las partes peligrosas. Luego se incluye en la ecuación el comportamiento humano: es necesario alentar a la gente a actuar con prudencia. Esos dos planteamientos se combinan de forma natural, y en ellos se han centrado a lo largo de los años unas campañas de educación que se han traducido en reducciones sustanciales del número de accidentes en el lugar de trabajo. Los carteles han tenido un papel fundamental en la propaganda sobre seguridad, terreno en el que han recurrido a un catálogo de mensajes simples y directos para manejar las herramientas y máquinas con seguridad, y ser prudentes en general en el lugar de trabajo. Los carteles presentados en este capítulo apelan a la responsabilidad personal del trabajador, a su sentido de la integridad física, a la camaradería, y a menudo también a la responsabilidad hacia la propia familia.

Además, se parecen todos mucho, independientemente de dónde se hayan difundido. En China y la India los trabajadores pueden ver atrapada su ropa por las máquinas no protegidas, y sufrir así los mismos accidentes horribles de que son escenario las fábricas europeas o estadounidenses. Pero lamentablemente, como ocurre con la riqueza, los riesgos para la seguridad también se distribuyen de forma desigual. El número de accidentes laborales es mayor en los países en desarrollo, donde la pobreza y la falta de protección jurídica se confabulan para relegar las cuestiones de seguridad en la agenda relacionada con los lugares de trabajo.

El movimiento en pro de la seguridad se inscribe además en un empeño más amplio de protección del conjunto de la sociedad. Así, no es de extrañar que se diseñen mensajes comparables en materia de seguridad vial, salud y prevención de incendios. También en el seno del hogar hay que ser prudente, y hoy día existen organismos que se dedican a informar a los ciudadanos sobre la mejor manera de garantizar la seguridad en el entorno doméstico. En muchas partes del mundo estos planteamientos han tenido un efecto positivo en la vida de numerosas personas; pero también se reconoce cada vez más -como ilustran algunos de los carteles- que actualmente la seguridad presenta aspectos que van más allá de la simple negligencia, en la que tanto hincapié se hacía en el pasado. ¿En qué peligros piensa la gente que tiene armas de fuego en su casa? ¿Qué sentido tiene pedir protección para no respirar aire contaminado en una fábrica cuando cualquier otra forma de contaminación puede llegar desde muy lejos hasta el hogar?

Обеспечьте безопасность. Соблюдайте! Избегайте! Делайте так! Не делайте! Соблюдайте процедуру! По мере развития промышленности в обществе люди рано или поздно осознают риски, связанные с их новой средой, и безопасность становится желаемой целью.

Обычно она начинается на предприятиях с внедрения более безопасных машин, защищающих пользователей от опасных частей. Затем в уравнение включается поведение человека: самих людей необходимо поощрять к безопасному поведению. Эти два подхода объединяются естественным образом и в течение ряда лет они были в центре просветительских кампаний, которые привели к значительному сокращению числа несчастных случаев на рабочем месте. Плакаты играли ключевую роль в пропаганде безопасности, используя простые сообщения о том, как безопасно обращаться с инструментом и работать на станках, а также в целом проявлять осторожность на рабочем месте. Представленные в этой главе плакаты взывают к личной ответственности работника, к физической самозащите, товариществу, а также часто к ответственности за свою семью.

Все они очень похожи, несмотря на то, в какой части мира они изготовлены. Как китайская, так и индийская одежда может попасть в незащищенную часть машины и привести к таким же ужасным несчастным случаям, какие происходили на предприятиях Европы или Америки. Но, к сожалению, так же, как и в отношении богатства, риски, связанные с безопасностью, распределены неравномерно. Число профессиональных несчастных случаев является гораздо большим в развивающихся странах, где бедность и отсутствие правовой защиты заставляют переместить вопросы безопасности на последнее место.

Движение за безопасность является частью более широкого движения за защиту всего общества. Неудивительно, что мы видим развитие сравнимых сообщений о дорожной безопасности, здоровье и защите от пожаров. У себя дома также лучше быть в безопасности, и поэтому сейчас созданы учреждения, которые объясняют отдельным гражданам, как добиться безопасности в быту. Во многих частях мира этот подход оказал положительное воздействие на жизнь многих людей; но в то же время растет осознание (проиллюстрированное на ряде плакатов) того, что вопросы безопасности сегодня являются гораздо более сложными, чем простое проявление осторожности, которое было в центре внимания в прошлом. От какой опасности люди хотят защититься, храня дома оружие? Какой смысл требовать защиты от загрязненного воздуха на предприятии, если загрязнение может быть принесено в дом издалека?

保证安全。服从！避免！了解！做到！不要做！遵守程序！社会走向工业化之时，人们迟早会了解到新环境具有的危险，保证安全就成了理想目标。

通常情况下，当工厂引进了较为安全的机器，能够保护使用者免受危险部件带来的伤害，安全问题就出现了。之后，人的行为就成了影响因素：需要鼓励人们采取安全行为。这两种方式自然地结合在一起，多年来也一直是宣教活动的重点，从而使工作场所的事故数量得到了大幅度减少。海报利用简单 的主题内容，告知人们如何安全地使用工具和操纵机器，以及一般情况下在工作场所如何谨慎工作，由此使得海报在安全宣传方面发挥着主要作用。本章节中的海报提请注意工人的个人责任、自我身体保护、同志关系，还有经常提到的个人家庭责任。

无论在世界的什么地方，海报看起来也非常相近。中国人和印度人的衣服都可能被没有任何防护的机器卷住，从而发生与欧洲或美洲的工厂同样的可怕事故。但遗憾的是，与财富一样，安全危险的分布也不够均匀。发展中国家发生的职业事故数目更大，贫穷和法律保护的缺失凑在一起，把安全问题推到了工作场所议程的后面。

安全运动是保护广大社会所做出的更大努力的组成部分。因此，当我们看到交通安全、健康和防火方面逐步形成的主题信息具有可比性，也就不足为奇了。在私密的家里，最好也要保证安全。现在已经成立了有关机构，告知各民众怎样实现家庭安全。在世界许多地方，这种方式对许多人的生活带来了积极影响。但是，正如一些海报所描述的那样，人们也越来越意识到，当今的安全问题与过去关注的简单疏忽大意相比更加深远。人们在家里藏枪到底要抵抗何种危险呢？污染物可以从远处刮进你的居家，如果在工厂里呼吸到的是不洁空气，要求保护又有何用呢？

حافظوا على سلامتكم. امتثلوا! تجنبوا! احترسوا! افعلوا! لا تفعلوا! اتبعوا الإجراءات! إن المجتمع عندما يتحول إلى مجتمع صناعي يدرك عاجلاً أم آجلاً المخاطر المحدقة به في بيئته الجديدة وتصبح السلامة من أهدافه المنشودة.

ويبدأ ذلك عادة في المصانع بإدخال آلات أكثر مأمونية تحمي المستخدم من الأجزاء الخطرة. وعندئذ يُصبح سلوك الإنسان طرفاً في المعادلة: فمن الضروري تشجيع الناس أنفسهم على أن يتوخوا السلامة في تصرفاتهم. وهذان الأسلوبان يمتزجان معا بشكل طبيعي وقد أصبحا، على مر السنين، محور تركيز حملات التوعية التي تمخضت عن خفض كبير لأعداد الحوادث التي تقع في أماكن العمل. وقد أدت الملصقات الإعلانية دوراً رئيسياً في الدعاية إلى السلامة، و ذلك باللجوء الى رسائل مبسطة بشأن مناولة الأدوات وتشغيل الآلات على نحو مأمون وتوخي الحرص. وقد دعت الملصقات الإعلانية المعروضة في هذا الفصل إلى المسؤولية الشخصية للعامل في ما يتعلق بالحفاظ على سلامته البدنية وعلى سلامة زملائه وأيضاً مسؤوليته عن أسرته في كثير من الأحيان.

وتبدو الملصقات الإعلانية متشابهة للغاية أيضاً بصرف النظر عن المكان الذي تأتي منه في العالم. فالملابس الصينية والهندية يمكن أن تعلق بالآلات غير المحمية مما يؤدي إلى الحوادث الرهيبة ذاتها التي تقع في مصانع أوروبا أو أمريكا. ولكن لسوء الحظ فإن المخاطر المحدقة بالسلامة ليست موزعة بالتساوي، شأنها شأن الثروة. فعدد الحوادث المهنية أعلى في البلدان النامية حيث يتضافر الفقر مع انعدام الحماية القانونية على بخس مكانة مسائل السلامة في برامج العمل الخاصة بأماكن العمل.

وتُشكل حركة السلامة، جزءاً من مبادرة أوسع من أجل حماية المجتمع بمعناه الأعم. لذا فلا عجب في أن نرى رسائل متشابهة تتطور بشأن سلامة المرور على الطرق والصحة والوقاية من الحرائق. وفي المنزل، وهو المكان الذي نتمتع فيه بخصوصيتنا، من الأفضل أيضاً أن نظل سالمين وهناك الآن وكالات قائمة بهدف إبلاغ المواطنين الأفراد بكيفية تحقيق السلامة في المنزل. وفي أنحاء عديدة من العالم كان لهذا الأسلوب أثر إيجابي في حياة كثير من الناس، ولكن هناك أيضاً إدراكاً متزايداً يتضح من بعض الملصقات الإعلانية، لأن مسائل السلامة أصبحت في هذه الأيام أعمق من مجرد تناول مسألة اللامبالاة والتي كانت محور التركيز في الماضي. فما المخاطر التي يسعى الناس إلى مواجهتها من خلال الاحتفاظ بمسدساتهم في منازلهم؟ وما فائدة طلب الحماية من استنشاق الهواء غير النقي في أي مصنع عندما يمكن للتلوث أن يقتحم علينا منازلنا من بعيد؟

Be Safe, Not Sorry

In the Wrong Hands, A Firearm can Change the Future
UNLOAD IT AND LOCK IT UP!

Center to Prevent Handgun Violence
1225 Eye Street, N.W.
Suite 1100
Washington, DC 20005
(202) 289-7319

www.cphv.org

■ Mieux vaut prévenir ce qu'on ne pourra pas guérir. Ne pas laisser traîner une arme à feu – Enlever les munitions et la mettre sous clé. ■ Más vale ser precavido que lamentarse después. Un arma de fuego que cae en manos equivocadas puede truncar el futuro: asegúrese de que su arma no va cargada y guárdela bajo llave. ■ Бережёного Бог бережёт. В плохих руках огнестрельное оружие может изменить всю жизнь. Разрядите и заприте его! ■ 要安全，不要遗憾：被拿在错误的手里，武器会改变未来：退出子弹，并锁住！

■ حافظ على سلامة طفلك كي لا تندم: السلاح الناري حين يمسك به الشخص غير المناسب يمكن أن يغير المستقبل: أفرغه من الذخيرة وحرزه!

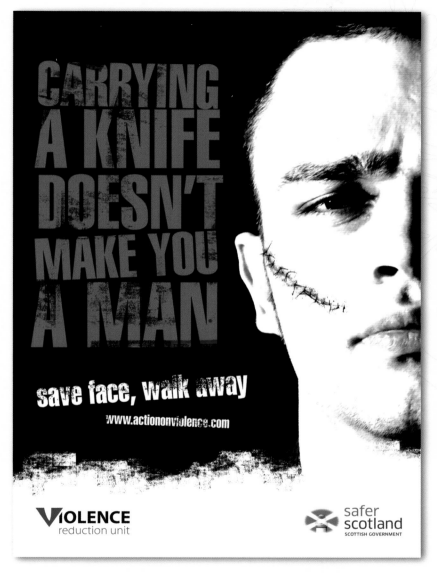

■ Ce n'est pas parce que tu as un couteau que tu es un homme. Sauve la face et passe ton chemin. ■ No eres más hombre por llevar encima un cuchillo. Mantén la calma y aléjate. ■ Нож при себе не делает вас настоящим мужчиной. Лучше уйти. ■ 携带刀子，并不能使你成为一名真正男子。为了颜面，一走了之。

■ إن حمل سكين لا يمكن أن يصنع منك رجلاً. حافظ على سلامة وجهك وابتعد.

113

■ Respect the highway code and uphold public order. ■ Respecte le code de la route et l'ordre public. ■ Observe el Código de Circulación y respete el orden público. ■ Соблюдай правила дорожного движения, поддерживай общественный порядок.

■ Be disciplined and ensure traffic safety. ■ Respecter la discipline améliore la sécurité routière. ■ Observe la disciplina de tráfico y contribuya a la seguridad vial. ■ Соблюдай дисциплину и обеспечивай безопасность транспортного движения.

■ Fais attention, car les doigts ne repoussent pas. ■ Ya que no puedes cultivar dedos, al menos cultiva la prudencia. ■ Новые пальцы вырастить невозможно, но проявлять большую осторожность можно. ■ 手指不能接种，所以开始就要当心。

■ احرص على سلامة أصابعك فإنها لا تعوض.

■ Juste une égratignure, mais mieux vaut désinfecter tout de suite pour éviter l'infection. ■ Es sólo un rasguño, pero… La dispensación inmediata de primeros auxilios previene muchas infecciones.
■ "Всего лишь царапина"… но! Инфекции можно избежать, оказав первую помощь. ■ "仅仅是一点擦伤"，可是即刻得到急救人员帮助，可预防感染！

■ «خدش بسيط» ولكن! لابد من تجنب العدوى بفضل الإسعافات الأولية.

■ Mind that hole! ■ Ne tombe pas dedans ! ■ ¡Cuidado con ese agujero! ■ Не попади туда! ■ 小心洞穴！

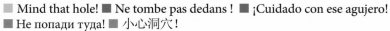

■ إياكم والسقوط هنا.

■ Don't smoke in bed. ■ Ne fume pas au lit ! ■ ¡No fumes en la cama! ■ Не кури в постели! ■ 请不要在床上吸烟。

■ لا تدخن في السرير.

■ Last year, 1000 people were killed and 25 000 were injured on the roads. Do you want to join them? The highway code applies to you also. ■ L' an dernier, il y a eu 1000 morts et 25 000 blessés sur les routes … Tu veux les rejoindre ? Piétons, le code de la route vous concerne aussi. ■ El año pasado hubo 1000 muertos y 25 000 heridos en las carreteras. ¿Quieres sumarte a ellos? Respeta el Código de la Circulación. ■ В прошлом году 1000 человек погибли и 25 000 получили травмы на дорогах… Ты хочешь к ним присоединиться? Пешеходы, правила дорожного движения касаются и вас! ■ 去年，1000人死于道路交通事故，25000人受伤。你想成为其中的一员吗？你也应该遵守公路法规。

■ في العام الماضي قضى 1000 شخص نحبه وأصيب 25000 شخص علي الطرق.........
هل تريد أن تكون الضحية التالية؟ أيها المارة إن قانون المرور يعنيكم أيضاً !

■ Protect your eyes. ■ Protège tes yeux ! ■ Protege tus ojos. ■ Берегите глаза. ■ 保护好你的眼睛。

■ حافظوا على سلامة أعينكم.

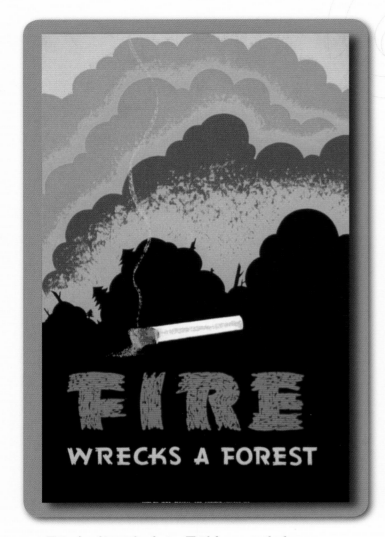

FIRE
WRECKS A FOREST

■ Le feu détruit les forêts. ■ El fuego puede destrozar un bosque entero. ■ Огонь губит лес. ■ 火灾毁灭森林。
■ الحرائق تدمر الغابات.

laat een eindje geen BEGIN zijn

■ Let's hope your cigarette ends don't start something. ■ Que la fin de ta cigarette ne soit pas le début d'autre chose. ■ Esperemos que el final de tu cigarrillo no sea el principio de otra cosa. ■ Как бы конец сигареты на стал началом чего-то другого. ■ 但愿你用过的烟头，不要点燃其他物品。

■ نرجو ألا يتسبب عقب السيجارة في بداية شيء آخر.

118

■ Gear wheels must be covered. ■ Couvrir les roues dentées.
■ No deje las ruedas dentadas al descubierto. ■ Шестерни
должны быть закрыты.

■ لابد من تغطية العجلات ذات التروس.

■ For your safety - don't wear loose clothes. ■ Pour ta sécurité, ne
porte pas de vêtements trop amples. ■ Por su seguridad, no lleve
prendas holgadas. ■ Для вашей же безопасности - не носите
слишком свободную одежду! ■ 为了你的安全——不要穿宽松
衣服。

■ لأجل سلامتك حافظ على ملابسك.

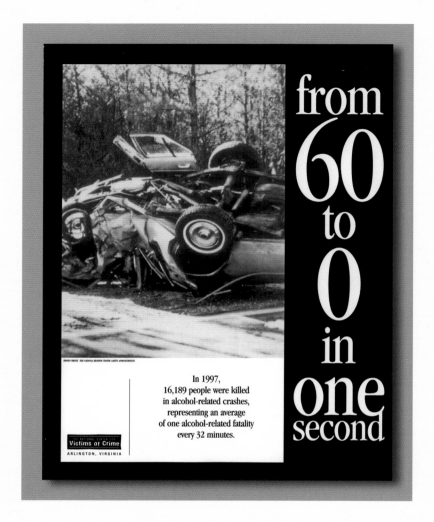

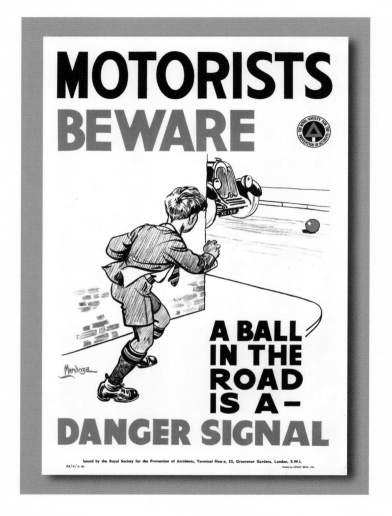

■ De 60 à 0 en une seconde. ■ Pasó de 60 a 0 millas en un segundo. ■ С 60 до 0 км в час - за одну секунду. ■ 从60到0，仅用一秒钟。

■ من 60 إلى صفر في ثانية واحدة.

■ Automobilistes attention ! Un ballon sur la route est un signe de danger. ■ Atención conductor: una pelota en la calzada es una señal de peligro. ■ Автомобилисты, будьте внимательны: мяч на дороге - сигнал опасности. ■ 司机们请注意：路上遇见皮球是危险的标志。

■ يا سائقي المركبات توخوا الحرص. وجود كرة في الطريق علامة خطيرة.

VOUS ÊTES JUSTE PASSÉ À L'ORANGE,
IL PASSERA JUSTE SA VIE À L'HÔPITAL.

www.securite-routiere.gouv.fr

SÉCURITÉ
ROUTIÈRE

CHANGEONS

You just went through the amber light. He'll spend the rest of his life in hospital. ■ Usted sólo pasó el semáforo en ámbar. Él pasará el resto de su vida en el hospital. ■ Вы "всего лишь" проскочили на желтый, он "всего лишь" проведет жизнь в больнице. ■ 你仅闯过了黄灯：他要在医院度过余生。

■ لقد تحركت والإشارة برتقالية ونجوت. أما هو فسيقضي بقية حياته في المستشفى.

En retard ?

La vitesse peut tuer tous les usagers de la route qu'ils soient conducteurs, piétons ou cyclistes. Une diminution de 5% de la vitesse moyenne peut entraîner une réduction de 30% du nombre d'accidents mortels.
Agis: lève le pied.

L'ACCIDENT DE LA ROUTE N'EST PAS UNE FATALITE

www.who.int/roadsafety

■ Running late? ■ ¿Lleva usted prisa? ■ Опоздал? ■ 要迟到了吗？

■ هل تأخرت عن الموعد؟

What about your helmet?
¿Y el casco? ■ А каска?
戴头盔了吗?
هل لبست خوذتك ؟

Et le casque ?
Les conducteurs de deux-roues meurent le plus souvent de blessures
à la tête. Le port du casque peut réduire de 40% le risque de décès et
de 70% le risque de blessures graves.
Agis: mets ton casque.

www.who.int/roadsafety

Être vu ?
Parfois peu visibles sur les routes, les piétons et les cyclistes sont
vulnérables. Si tu portes des vêtements clairs ou réfléchissants,
tu es plus visible et tu risques moins une collision.
Agis: fais-toi voir sur la route.

www.who.int/roadsafety

Make sure you can be seen.
¿Visible para los demás?
Тебя видно?
确保别人能看到你。
على أن يراك الناس.
احرص.

What about your safety belt?
¿Y el cinturón de seguridad?
А ремень безопасности?
系上安全带了吗?
هل ربطت حزام الأمان؟

Et la ceinture ?
Le port de la ceinture diminue de 40% à 65% le risque
de mourir ou d'être gravement blessé en cas d'accident.
Agis: mets ta ceinture.

www.who.int/roadsafety

Trop bu ?
Boire de l'alcool avant de conduire augmente le risque d'accident et la probabilité de
mourir ou d'être gravement blessé. En adoptant une loi contre l'alcool au volant et en
la faisant respecter, on peut diminuer de 20% le nombre de tués sur les routes.
Agis: ne bois jamais d'alcool avant de conduire.

www.who.int/roadsafety

Had too much to drink?
¿Demasiado alcohol?
Слишком много выпил?
饮酒过多了吗?
هل أسرفت في الشرب ؟

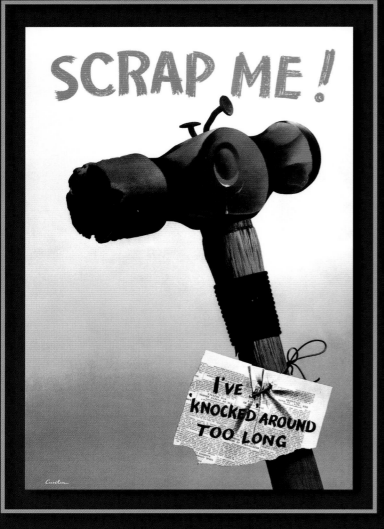

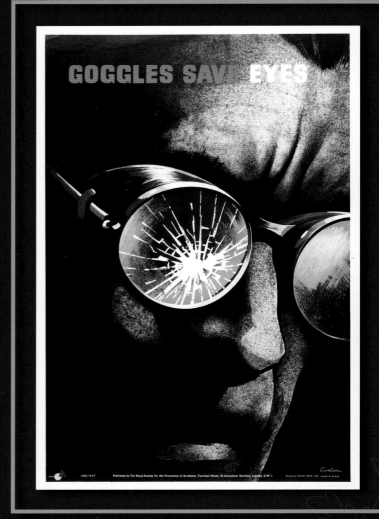

■ En voilà un qui n'a que trop servi ! ■ ¡Tírame a la basura! Ya llevo demasiado tiempo martilleando clavos. ■ Сдай меня в металлолом! Я слишком долго работал. ■ 废掉我吧！我敲打的时间够长了。

■ تخلص مني كخردة فقد استخدمت في الطَرق لمدة طويلة.

■ Les lunettes de protection peuvent sauver la vue.
■ Las lentes protectoras pueden salvarle la vista.
■ Очки защищают глаза. ■ 护目镜可以保护眼睛。
■ النظارة الواقية تحافظ على سلامة العينين.

■ If you don't want to finish up like this, exercise your right to solve the problem. ■ Si tu ne veux pas que cela t'arrive, utilise ton droit pour résoudre le problème. ■ Si no quieres que las cosas sean así, haz valer tus derechos para resolver el problema. ■ Не хотите оказаться в такой ситуации - реализуйте свое право решать проблемы. ■ 如果你不希望这样–那就利用你的权利，去解决问题。

■ إذا لم تشأ أن يحدث لك هذا فعليك باستعمال حقك في حل المشكلة.

■ Une rupture ici et c'est peut-être la mort plus bas. Sécurité d'abord.
■ Si algo falla en el aire, alguien puede morir en la calle. La seguridad es lo primero. ■ Проблема здесь - смерть внизу. Безопасность прежде всего! ■ 这里出了问题，下面的人可能会丧命。安全第一。

■ الفشل هنا قد يعني الموت أسفل هذا الحمل السلامة قبل كل شيء.

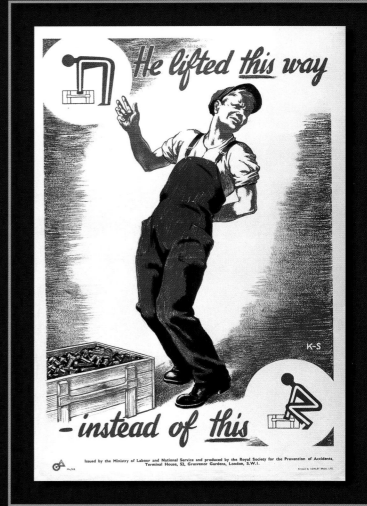

■ Stop! Hearing protection needed! Use earplugs at least. Avoid becoming deaf! ■ Halte ! Ici il faut se protéger contre le bruit pour ne pas devenir sourd. Utilise au moins des bouchons d'oreilles! ■ ¡Alto! En este lugar hay que protegerse contra el ruido, por lo menos con tapones de oídos. Evite la sordera. ■ Стоп! Надо защитить органы слуха, по крайней мере с помощью берушей. Иначе вы оглохнете! ■ 暂停一下！需要保护听力。至少带上耳塞，以防造成耳聋! ■ توقفوا! حماية السمع ضرورية هنا. استعملوا سدادات الأذن على الأقل. تجنبوا الإصابة بالصمم.

■ Il l'a soulevée comme cela, alors qu'il aurait fallu le faire comme ceci. ■ Intentó levantar la caja así en lugar de así. ■ Он поднял груз так, а не так. ■ 他这样搬物，而不像这样。 ■ لقد رفع الحمل هكذا بدلا من هذه الطريقة.

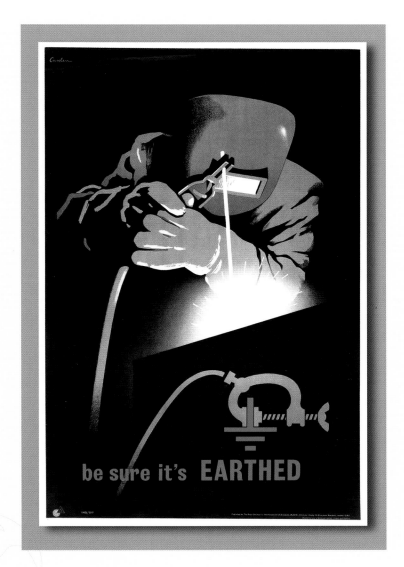

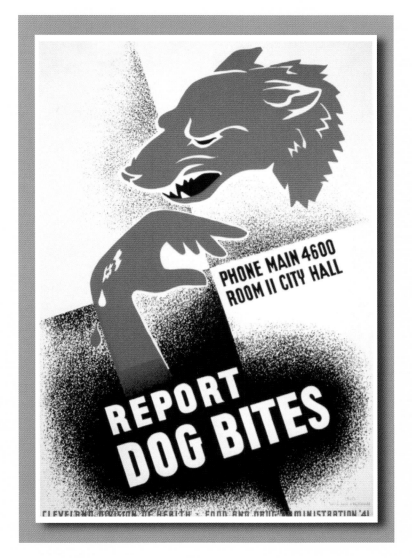

■ Attention à la mise à terre. ■ Asegúrese de que está conectado a tierra. ■ Проверь, есть ли заземление. ■ 要确保地线接地。

■ تأكد من التوصيلات الأرضية.

■ Signaler toute morsure de chien. ■ Notifique los casos de mordeduras de perro. ■ Сообщайте об укусах собак. ■ 被狗咬伤了，请报告。

■ أبلغ عن عضة الكلب.

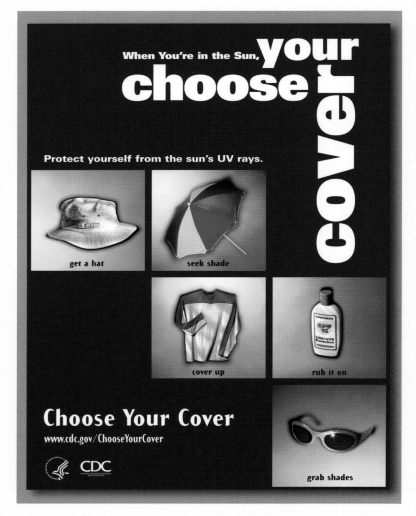

■ Si t'es bronzé, t'es grillé. Le bronzage ou le coup de soleil entraînent des lésions de la peau. Choisis ta protection. ■ Una piel bronceada es una piel tostada. Quemadura o bronceado: ambos son sinónimos de piel dañada. Escoja la protección más indicada para usted. ■ Загорел - значит обгорел. Сильный загар, или солнечный ожог, - это поврежденная кожа. Лучше накрыться. ■ 晒黑了，倒霉的是你。晒黑或晒伤-就是皮肤损伤。选择你的遮护方式。

■ إذا سفع جلدك فقد تحمصت. التعرض للسفع أو حروق الشمس يعني تلف الجلد. اختر غطاءك.

■ Au soleil, choisis ta protection. ■ Para las exposiciones solares ... escoja la protección más indicada para usted. ■ Вышел на солнце - защитись. ■ 在阳光中，请选择你的遮护方式。

■ اختر غطاءك عندما تتعرض للشمس.

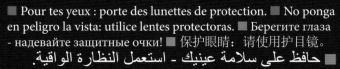

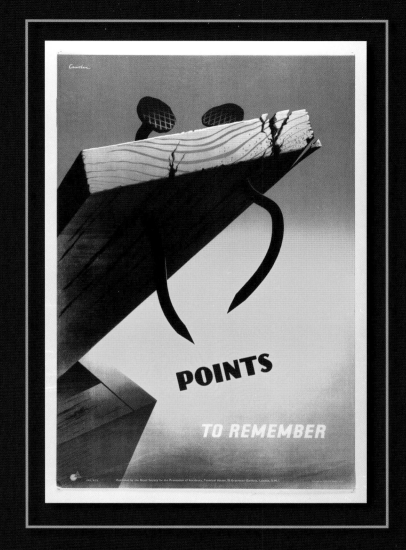

■ Pour tes yeux : porte des lunettes de protection. ■ No ponga en peligro la vista: utilice lentes protectoras. ■ Берегите глаза - надевайте защитные очки! ■ 保护眼睛：请使用护目镜。

■ حافظ على سلامة عينيك ـ استعمل النظارة الواقية.

■ Attention aux clous. ■ Cuidado con las puntas. ■ Помни об осторожности! ■ 当心这些尖物。

■ كلاليب لابد من الحذر منها.

ممارسة
الرضاعة
الطبيعية

Allaiter

Amamantar

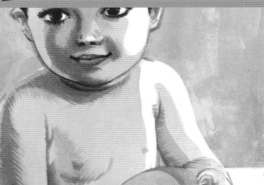

Обеспечьте
грудное
вскармливание

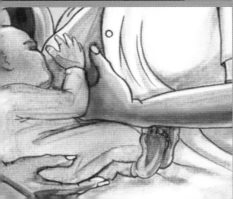

Breastfeed

母乳喂养

Breastfeed   A mother nurturing her child is a powerful image of health. The exposure of the breast – in illustration or in life – may be considered indiscreet in some cultures but there is no question that human milk creates a future generation that is strong and vital.

Breastfeeding – especially exclusive breastfeeding – keeps mothers and children healthy by providing an irreplaceable ability to fight disease. Breastfeeding saves the lives of children that would otherwise be lost to diarrhoea, pneumonia and many other infections and chronic diseases. The maternal consequences of breastfeeding include reduced anaemia, delayed return of fertility after birth, and a reduced risk of diabetes and breast and other cancers.

Over the years the themes in public health breastfeeding posters have changed from the simple message of "breast is best" to action messages supporting women in overcoming health, social and cultural barriers to successful breastfeeding. Newer posters illustrate issues that are important to public health and to health-minded individuals: stressing that breastfeeding is environmentally appropriate, life-saving, prevents disease and improves development. As this evolution continues, we may expect to see more images that underscore the risks when children are fed alternatives to human milk.

Why is there a need to actively promote such a natural and relatively common behaviour? Because the patterns of breastfeeding deteriorated worldwide in the last century partly due to aggressive marketing of infant formula to parents and health workers. Only now do we fully recognize that exclusive and continued breastfeeding – which is still relatively rare – is the most important single intervention that we should be supporting if we wish to achieve increases in child survival overall.

Breastfeeding is so much more than a beautiful symbol of motherhood. We need an agenda of protection, promotion and support to encourage this life-enhancing practice. Breastfeeding mothers need support through improved health systems, health worker education and community action. Families need legislation that allows maternity leave and workplace feeding, and that prevents the use of misleading information that promotes breast milk substitutes.

The UNICEF/WHO Baby-friendly Hospital Initiative and the WHO *International Code of Marketing of Breast-milk Substitutes* provide such guidance. These initiatives have supported health worker education and improved maternity practices in more than 150 countries and applied public pressure on infant-formula manufacturers to stop misleading and false advertising, direct marketing to the public and provision of free samples and incentives. The Code has been implemented to some extent in more than 80 countries.

Allaiter.   Une mère donnant le sein à son enfant, quelle belle image de santé ! Si dans certaines cultures le sein ne saurait être exposé, que ce soit sur une illustration ou dans la vie réelle, il ne fait aucun doute que le lait maternel contribue à la force et à la vitalité de la génération future.

L'allaitement maternel – surtout l'allaitement exclusif – donne à la mère et à l'enfant une capacité irremplaçable de lutte contre la maladie; il sauve la vie d'enfants qui sans cela succomberaient à une diarrhée, à une pneumonie ou d'autres maladies infectieuses et chroniques. Pour la mère, il réduit l'anémie et entraîne un retour plus tardif à la fécondité et un risque plus faible de diabète et de certains cancers, notamment de cancer du sein.

Au fil des années, les thèmes des affiches consacrées à l'allaitement maternel sont passés du message simple du type « le lait maternel est le meilleur » à des messages actifs aidant les femmes à surmonter les obstacles sanitaires, sociaux et culturels à un allaitement harmonieux. Les affiches plus récentes illustrent des questions importantes pour la santé publique et pour les individus préoccupés par la santé, soulignant que l'allaitement est favorable à l'environnement, qu'il permet de sauver des vies et d'éviter des maladies. Alors que cette évolution se poursuit, nous pouvons nous attendre à voir d'autres images qui soulignent les risques encourus lorsque l'enfant reçoit autre chose que du lait maternel.

Pourquoi faut-il promouvoir un comportement aussi naturel et relativement courant ? Parce que la situation s'est dégradée au cours du siècle dernier dans le monde entier en partie à la suite de la commercialisation agressive des fabricants de préparations pour nourrissons auprès des parents et des soignants. Ce n'est qu'aujourd'hui que nous reconnaissons pleinement que l'allaitement exclusif et continu – encore relativement rare – est l'intervention la plus importante que nous devrions favoriser si nous voulons améliorer le taux de survie de l'enfant d'une manière générale.

L'allaitement maternel est beaucoup plus qu'un symbole éclatant de la maternité. Nous avons besoin d'un programme de protection, de promotion et de soutien pour encourager cette pratique favorable à la vie. Les mères allaitantes doivent pouvoir compter sur de meilleurs systèmes de santé, sur des agents de santé mieux formés et sur l'action communautaire. Les familles ont besoin d'une législation qui permette les congés maternité et l'allaitement au travail et qui empêche la diffusion d'informations erronées dans la promotion des substituts du lait maternel.

L'Initiative UNICEF/OMS des hôpitaux « amis des bébés » et le *Code international OMS de commercialisation des substituts du lait maternel* contiennent les lignes directrices nécessaires. Ces deux mesures on favorisé l'éducation du personnel de santé, amélioré les pratiques de maternité dans plus de 150 pays et ont permis d'exercer de pressions sur les fabricants de préparations pour nourrissons afin qu'ils renoncent à la diffusion d'annonces trompeuses, à la commercialisation directe auprès du public, à la distribution d'échantillons gratuits et à d'autres incitations. Le Code a été appliqué en partie dans plus de 80 pays.

Amamantar. La imagen de una madre alimentando a su hijo connota salud de forma poderosa. La exposición del pecho -de forma gráfica o en la vida real- se considera indiscreta en algunas culturas, pero no cabe duda de que la leche materna confiere fuerza y vitalidad a las futuras generaciones.

La lactancia natural, en especial como alimentación exclusiva, dotan a las madres y sus hijos de un arma irreemplazable para combatir las enfermedades. La lactancia materna salva vidas infantiles que de lo contrario se perderían como consecuencia de la diarrea o la neumonía, o de otras enfermedades infecciosas o crónicas. Entre los efectos del amamantamiento en la madre cabe citar una menor incidencia de anemia, el retraso de la recuperación de la fecundidad tras el nacimiento y un menor riesgo de diabetes y de diversos tipos de cáncer, en particular del de mama.

A lo largo de los años el contenido de los carteles dedicados a la lactancia natural ha evolucionado desde la simple idea de que dar el pecho es la mejor alternativa hasta mensajes de acción que apoyan a las mujeres para que superen las barreras sanitarias, sociales y culturales a una buena lactancia natural. Los carteles más recientes ilustran aspectos relevantes para la salud pública y para las personas preocupadas por su salud, resaltando que el amamantamiento es una opción apropiada desde el punto de vista ambiental, salva vidas y previene enfermedades. Considerando esa tendencia, cabe prever que veremos más imágenes resaltando los riesgos que entrañan para los niños los alimentos distintos de la leche materna.

¿Por qué es necesario promover un comportamiento natural y relativamente frecuente como es ése? La razón es que las prácticas de lactancia materna se deterioraron en todo el mundo durante el siglo pasado, en parte como consecuencia de una agresiva mercadotecnia, dirigida a los progenitores y los trabajadores sanitarios, de las preparaciones para lactantes. Sólo desde hace poco se reconoce plenamente que la lactancia natural exclusiva -aún relativamente rara- es la intervención única que más deberíamos apoyar para conseguir aumentar globalmente la supervivencia infantil.

La lactancia natural es mucho más que un hermoso símbolo de la maternidad. Necesitamos una agenda de protección, promoción y apoyo de esa forma de alimentación como práctica que salva vidas. Las madres lactantes necesitan el respaldo de unos sistemas de salud mejorados, de unos trabajadores sanitarios formados al efecto y de iniciativas comunitarias. Las familias necesitan medidas legislativas que posibiliten las bajas por maternidad y el amamantamiento en el lugar de trabajo, y que impidan la difusión de información engañosa en la promoción de sucedáneos de la leche materna.

La iniciativa UNICEF/OMS de «hospitales amigos del niño» y el *Código Internacional de Comercialización de Sucedáneos de la Leche Materna* de la OMS ofrecen ese tipo de orientación. Esas dos iniciativas han favorecido la formación de los agentes de salud, mejorado las prácticas de maternidad en más de 150 países, y han permitido presionar a los fabricantes de preparaciones para lactantes para que renuncien a difundir anuncios falsos o engañosos, la comercialización directa al público y el recurso a muestras gratuitas u otros incentivos. El Código se ha aplicado en alguna medida en más de 80 países.

Обеспечьте грудное вскармливание. Мать, кормящая своего ребенка, - это очень сильная иллюстрация здоровья. Вид женской груди - на иллюстрации или в жизни - может восприниматься нескромным в некоторых культурах, но нет никаких сомнений в том, что женское молоко необходимо для сильного и жизнеспособного будущего поколения.

Грудное вскармливание, особенно исключительное грудное вскармливание, сохраняет здоровье матери и ребенка и обеспечивает уникальную способность противостоять болезням. Грудное вскармливание спасает жизни детей, которые в противном случае могли бы быть потеряны в результате диареи, пневмонии, а также многих других инфекционных и хронических болезней. Последствия грудного вскармливания для матери включают уменьшение анемии, отсрочку фертильности после родов и снижение риска диабета, рака молочной железы и других видов рака.

За прошедшие годы темы плакатов общественного здравоохранения о грудном вскармливании изменились от простого сообщения о том, что «кормить грудью - лучше всего» к активным сообщениям, оказывающим поддержку женщинам в преодолении связанных со здоровьем, социальных и культурных препятствий для грудного вскармливания. Более новые плакаты иллюстрируют вопросы, являющиеся важными для общественного здравоохранения и заботящихся о своем здоровье людей, подчеркивая, что грудное вскармливание способствует сохранению окружающей среды, спасает жизнь, предупреждает болезни и способствует развитию. По мере дальнейшего развития в этом направлении мы, возможно, увидим больше изображений, подчеркивающих риски для детей, вскармливаемых альтернативными продуктами, а не грудным молоком.

Почему необходимо активно пропагандировать такое естественное и относительно распространенное поведение? Потому, что в течение последнего столетия показатели грудного вскармливания ухудшились во всем мире, отчасти из-за агрессивного маркетинга среди родителей и работников здравоохранения детских питательных смесей. Мы только сейчас полностью осознали, что исключительное длительное грудное вскармливание (которое все еще является относительно редким) является самой важной единственной мерой, которую нам следует поддерживать, чтобы добиться общего улучшения выживания детей.

Грудное вскармливание является гораздо большим, чем просто прекрасный символ материнства. Нам необходима повестка дня действий для защиты, поощрения и поддержки этой укрепляющей жизненные силы практики. Необходимо оказывать поддержку кормящим грудью матерям через улучшенные системы здравоохранения, посредством просвещения медико-санитарных работников и действий среди местного населения. Семьям необходимо законодательство, обеспечивающее отпуск по уходу за ребенком и возможность кормления на рабочем месте, а также предотвращающее использование вводящей в заблуждение информации, которая пропагандирует заменители грудного молока.

Инициатива ЮНИСЕФ-ВОЗ по поощрению в больницах грудного вскармливания и принятый ВОЗ Международный свод правил сбыта заменителей грудного молока обеспечивают такое руководство. Эти инициативы поддерживают просвещение работников здравоохранения, улучшенную практику материнства в более чем 150 странах и обеспечивают давление общественности на изготовителей детских смесей прекратить вводящую в заблуждение и обманную рекламу, прямой сбыт населению и предоставление бесплатных образцов и стимулов к приобретению. Этот Свод в той или иной степени применяется в 80 странах.

■ 母乳喂养。 一位养育孩子的母亲，就是一个强有力的健康图像。在演示时或在生活中暴露乳房，对有些文化而言可能算得上行为不检。但是，毫无疑问的是，人的乳汁创造了既强壮又充满活力的未来一代。

母乳喂养（特别是纯母乳喂养）可以增强抗击疾病的能力，这种能力是不可替换的，由此使得母亲和孩子保持健康状态。儿童可因腹泻病、肺炎以及许多其他传染病和慢性病丧命，母乳喂养则能够挽救儿童由此可能丧失的生命。母乳喂养对母亲带来的影响有：缓解贫血，推迟产后生育力的恢复，以及降低患糖尿病、乳腺癌和其它癌症的风险。

多年来，母乳喂养的公共卫生海报主题发生了变化，也就是由"最好的是乳房"这样的简单内容，改为支持妇女的行动内容，支持她们克服在实现母乳喂养过程中遇到的健康、社会和文化障碍。较新的海报展示对公共卫生和苛护健康者具有重要意义的问题：强调母乳喂养对环境有益，可以挽救生命，预防疾病，并且增进发育。如果这种演变持续下去，我们就可更多地看到强调孩子食用人乳代用品时所面临危险的海报。

为什么要积极促进这样一个既自然又相对常见的行为呢？原因是，在过去的一个世纪，世界范围内的母乳喂养方式出现了倒退。这在一定程度上是由于向父母和卫生工作者积极营销婴儿配方奶粉造成的。直到现在，我们才完全认识到，在持续性纯母乳喂养仍然相对稀少的情况下，如果要全面提高儿童的生存，我们必须支持纯母乳喂养这种单一且最重要的干预方法。

母乳喂养不仅仅是一个为母之道的美丽象征。我们需要一个保护、促进和支持性的议程，以鼓励这种能够延长生命的做法。通过改善卫生系统、卫生工作者教育和社区行动，为母乳喂养母亲提供所需要的支持。家庭要获得相应的法律，能够允许休产假并在工作场所喂养孩子，并要防止使用母乳替代品促销方面的误导信息。

联合国儿童基金会/世界卫生组织爱婴医院行动，以及世界卫生组织《国际母乳代用品销售守则》可以就此提供指导。在150多个国家，爱婴医院行动对卫生工作者的教育提供了支持，改善了产妇做法，同时公众对婴儿配方生产商造成了压力，使其停止进行令人产生误解并且虚假的广告宣传，不向公众进行直接营销，不提供免费样品和奖励方法。该守则在80多个国家得到了不同程度的实施。

ممارسة الرضاعة الطبيعية إن صورة الأم التي تغذي طفلها صورة مؤثرة من الصور. وقد يُعتبر عرض صورة الثدي في الأشكال التوضيحية أو صورة الثدي في الحياة العادية غير لائق في بعض الثقافات، ولكن ما من شك في أن لبن الأم يصنع جيلاً من أجيال المستقبل يتمتع بالقوة والحيوية.

والرضاعة الطبيعية، وخصوصاً إذا تم الاقتصار عليها، تجعل الأمهات والأطفال موفوري الصحة دائماً من خلال منحهم قدرة لا بديل لها على مكافحة المرض. فالرضاعة الطبيعية تنقذ أرواح الأطفال التي لولاها لتسبب الإسهال والالتهاب الرئوي وغير ذلك من حالات العدوى والأمراض المزمنة في القضاء عليها. ومن آثار الرضاعة الطبيعية على الأمومة تقليل الإصابة بفقر الدم وتأخير عودة الخصوبة بعد الولادة وتقليل مخاطر الإصابة بالسكري وسرطان الثدي والسرطانات الأخرى. وعلى مر السنين تغيرت المواضيع التي تناولتها الملصقات الإعلانية للرضاعة الطبيعية والمتعلقة بالصحة العمومية من مجرد رسالة «الرضاعة الطبيعية هي الأفضل» إلى رسائل عملية تدعم النساء في التغلب على العقبات الصحية والاجتماعية والثقافية التي تحول دون النجاح في ممارسة الرضاعة الطبيعية.

وتبين الملصقات الإعلانية الأحدث القضايا الهامة للصحة العمومية وللأفراد المعنيين بالصحة: ومن أمثلة ذلك التشديد على أن الرضاعة الطبيعية ملائمة بيئياً وتنفذ الحياة وتقي من الأمراض وتحسن النمو. ومع استمرار هذا التطور يجوز لنا أن نتوقع مشاهدة المزيد من الصور التي تركز على المخاطر التي تحدق بالأطفال عندما تتم تغذيتهم ببدائل لبن الأم.

ولكن لماذا يلزم الترويج بنشاط لسلوك طبيعي وشائع نسبياً كهذا؟ لأن أنماط الرضاعة الطبيعية تدهورت على نطاق العالم خلال القرن الماضي لأسباب منها التسويق العاتي لأغذية الرضّع لدى الوالدين والعاملين الصحيين. وقد أصبحنا نعترف اعترافاً تاماً الآن فحسب بأن الاقتصار على الرضاعة الطبيعية والاستمرار فيه، وهو الأمر النادر نسبياً الآن، هو أهم تدخل وحيد ينبغي لنا دعمه إذا كنا نريد زيادة بقاء الأطفال على قيد الحياة عموماً.

والرضاعة الطبيعية أوسع بكثير من أن تكون رمزاً جميلاً للأمومة. ونحن في حاجة إلى وضع برنامج عمل لحمايتها وتعزيزها ودعمها من أجل تشجيع هذه الممارسة التي تحسّن الحياة. والأمهات اللائي يُرضعن رضاعة طبيعية بحاجة إلى الدعم عن طريق تحسين النُظم الصحية وتوعية العاملين الصحيين واتخاذ الإجراءات اللازمة في المجتمع المحلي. كما أن الأسر في حاجة إلى سن تشريع يسمح بأخذ إجازة أمومة وبالإرضاع في أماكن العمل ويمنع استخدام المعلومات المضللة تروج لبدائل لبن الأم.

وتتاح هذه الإرشادات من خلال مبادرة المستشفيات المصادقة للرضّع المشتركة بين اليونيسيف ومنظمة الصحة العالمية وكذلك المدونة التي وضعتها المنظمة للقواعد الدولية لتسويق بدائل لبن الأم. وقد دعمت هذه المبادرات تثقيف العاملين الصحيين وتحسين ممارسات الأمومة في أكثر من 150 بلداً ومارست الضغوط على المدونة فتطالب صانعي أغذية الرضّع للتوقف عن بث الإعلانات المضللة والتي تنشر معلومات مضللة وغير صحيحة عن التسويق المباشر لدى الجمهور وعن إعطاء عينات مجانية وحوافز. وقد تم تنفيذ المدونة إلى حد ما في أكثر من 80 بلداً.

■ La collation gratuite et rapide pour bébé. ■ Comida rápida – y gratuita – para los bebés. ■ Самое быстрое и бесплатное питание для грудных детей. ■ 宝宝的免费快餐。
■ غذاء سريع ومجاني للرضّع.

■ Breastfeeding: what could be more natural. ■ Lactancia materna: no hay nada más natural. ■ Материнское молоко - что может более естественным. ■ 母乳喂养：最合乎自然的方式。
■ رضاعة الأم لا تجافي الفطرة.

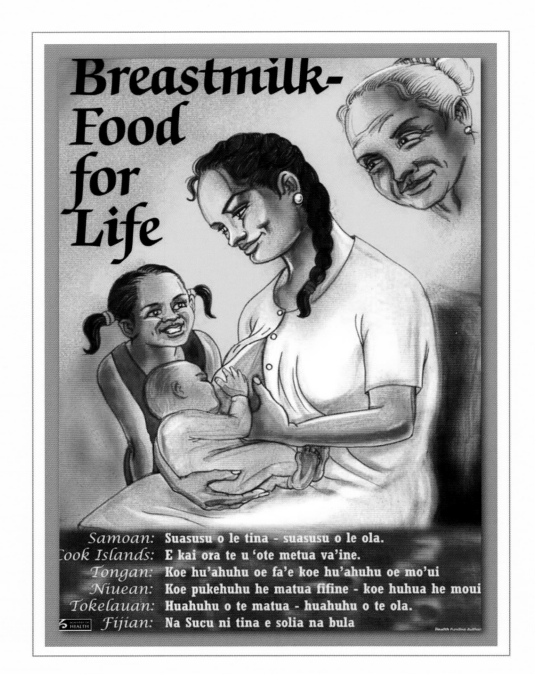

■ Le lait maternel : une nourriture pour la vie. ■ Dar el pecho es apostar por la vida. ■ Грудное молоко - питание на всю жизнь. ■ 母乳——维系生命的食物。

■ لبن الأم غذاء من أجل الحياة.

136

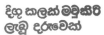

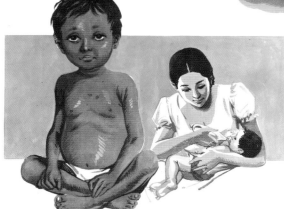

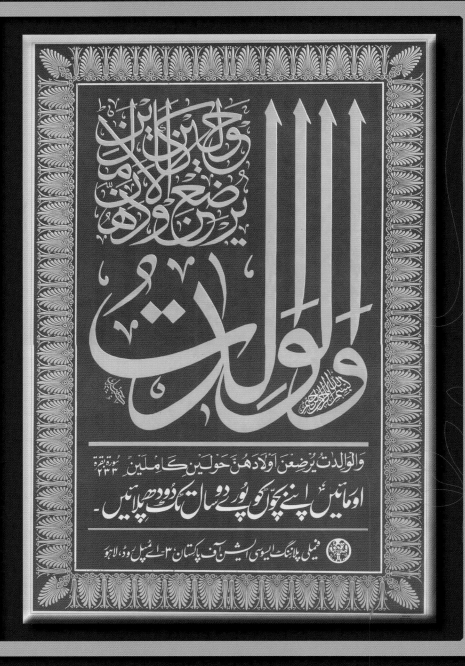

Mothers shall breastfeed their offspring for two whole years. ■ La mère allaitera son enfant pendant deux années entières. ■ Las madres amamantarán a sus hijos durante dos años completos. ■ Матери должны вскармливать грудью своих детей в течение двух полных лет. ■ 母亲用母乳喂养孩子要有两整年。

■ A quote from the Quran stating that two years is the maximum duration for breastfeeding, if the father so wishes. ■ Une citation d'un verset du Coran: «La mère allaitera son enfant pendant deux années entières, si le père le décide.» ■ Cita de un pasaje del Corán que prevé que las madres amamantarán a sus hijos durante dos años completos, si así lo desea el padre. ■ Цитата из Корана, где говорится, что 2 года - это максимальный срок для грудного вскармливания при условии желания отца. ■ 引用《古兰经》话说，根据父亲意愿，母乳喂养最长可持续两年。

■ Breastfeeding versus bottle-feeding. ■ Allaitement au sein ou au biberon? ■ Lactancia materna frente a alimentación con biberón. ■ Грудное вскармливание в противовес искусственному. ■ 母乳喂养与奶瓶喂养。

■ الرضاعة الطبيعية بدلاً من التغذية من القارورة.

Le lait maternel est l'aliment le plus nutritif. ■ La leche materna es la más nutritiva. ■ Грудное молоко - самое питательное! 母乳最具营养。

■ لبن الأم أغنى غذاء.

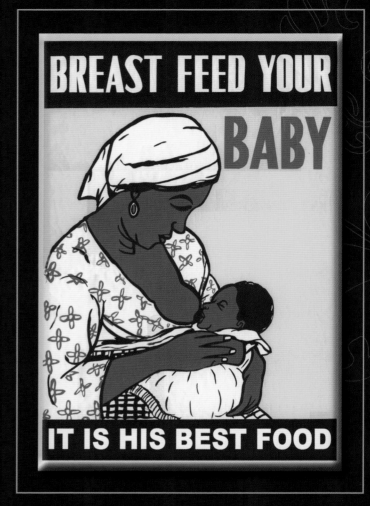

■ Allaite ton enfant. C'est ce qu' il y a de mieux pour lui. ■ Amamante a su bebé. No hay mejor alimento que la leche materna. ■ Вскармливайте грудью вашего младенца. Это самое лучшее питание. ■ 用母乳喂养你的孩子。 这是孩子的最佳食物。

■ أرضعن أطفالكن من أثدائكن. هذا أفضل غذاء لهم.

■ To preserve breastfeeding ... like water, air and the earth ... is to preserve life. ■ Préserver l'allaitement maternel ... comme l'eau, l'air et la terre … c'est préserver la vie.
■ Охрана грудного вскармливания - это, так же как охрана воды, воздуха и земли, охрана жизни. ■ 像保护水、空气和土壤一样，保持母乳喂养就是保全生命。
■ الحفاظ على الرضاعة الطبيعية مثل الحفاظ على الماء والهواء والأرض... إنه حفاظ على الحياة.

كلوا وتحركوا

Manger
et bouger

Manger
et bouger

Eat and move

Comer y
moverse

吃与动

Ешьте и
двигайтесь

Eat and move. The posters in this chapter show very clearly that historical events and social factors change the messages spread by public health officials. War, rationing and economic downturn in Europe in the first half of the 20th century are reflected in the instructions to clean your plate and eat nationally-produced food; "Corn: the food of the nation". Even the science which informs these posters has been affected by conflict. Between the two World Wars, the United States of America and many European nations took part in extensive research into the effects of diet and exercise on health. New understandings emerged about the quality and quantities of food needed to maintain health, in particular the essential role of vitamins. This is why several of the posters recommend specific types of food, for example oranges or fish oil. Warfare concentrates the attention of governments on the health and strength of their populations. In peacetime, sporting events allow nations to demonstrate the strength and physical achievement of their young adults and we can see this pride reflected in posters from China, Ukraine and the USA.

Most of the posters about eating offer essentially the same advice – a mixed, balanced diet – but they are illustrated with different foods. Posters which rely on a strong visual image rather than written instructions have to be carefully designed to suit local cultures. This is an important lesson for public health authorities dealing with refugee or immigrant populations, when the usual posters show foods that new residents cannot recognize or would not eat. There is also a tension in different countries between those who have too much and those who have too little. In the 20th century the diseases of excess have gradually proved to be as deadly as those of deprivation; it can seem very strange to advise people to eat and move, activities which we expect to come naturally.

Yet different people need different lifestyles to maintain health, and therefore advice about diet and exercise is increasingly individualized. Exercise that is exhilarating for one person might cause infarct or injury in another (and swimming in a dirty pool is dangerous for everyone!). The caloric requirement for a woman doing hard physical labour is not the same as that for a man who does a sedentary job. These issues pose challenges to poster designers – so both the health message *and* the pictures used to illustrate that message need to be carefully chosen.

Manger et bouger. Les affiches de ce chapitre montrent très clairement que les événements historiques et les facteurs sociaux modifient les messages diffusés par les responsables de la santé publique. La guerre, le rationnement et la crise économique que l'Europe a connus au cours de la première moitié du XXe siècle sont reflétés dans l'ordre de finir ce qu'il y a dans notre assiette et de consommer des produits nationaux. Même la science qui a contribué à la mise au point de ces affiches a été touchée par le conflit. Entre les deux guerres mondiales, les Etats-Unis d'Amérique et de nombreux pays européens ont fait d'importantes recherches sur les effets du régime alimentaire et de l'activité physique sur la santé. De nouvelles conceptions sont apparues concernant la qualité et la quantité des aliments nécessaires pour préserver la santé, notamment le rôle essentiel des vitamines. C'est pour cela que plusieurs des affiches recommandent des aliments particuliers, par exemple les oranges ou l'huile de foie de morue. Les situations de guerre amènent les pouvoirs publics à réfléchir à la santé et à la force de la population. En temps de paix, des manifestations sportives permettent aux nations de montrer les capacités et les succès physiques des jeunes adultes ; on observe ce genre de fierté dans les affiches de la Chine, des Etats-Unis et de l'Ukraine.

La plupart des affiches concernant la façon de se nourrir donnent essentiellement le même conseil : privilégier un régime alimentaire varié et équilibré, mais différents aliments figurent dans les illustrations. Les affiches qui mettent l'accent sur l'image plutôt que sur le texte doivent être soigneusement conçues de manière à tenir compte de la culture locale. C'est là un élément important dont les services de santé publique doivent tenir compte face à des populations de réfugiés ou d'immigrants lorsque les affiches habituelles illustrent des aliments que les nouveaux résidents ne reconnaissent pas ou ne consommeraient pas. Il existe aussi des tensions dans différents pays entre ceux qui ont trop et ceux qui n'ont pas assez. Au cours du XXe siècle, les maladies liées à la suralimentation sont progressivement devenues aussi mortelles que celles dues aux privations : il peut sembler bizarre de conseiller aux gens de manger et de bouger, des activités qui peuvent sembler naturelles.

Pourtant, différentes personnes ont besoin de modes de vie différents pour rester en bonne santé et, par conséquent, les conseils en matière de régime alimentaire et d'activité physique deviennent de plus en plus individualisés. Une activité soutenue bienfaisante pour l'un pourrait provoquer un traumatisme ou un infarctus chez l'autre (nager dans une piscine sale est dangereux pour n'importe qui !). Les besoins protéino-énergétiques d'une femme astreinte à un travail physiquement pénible sont supérieurs à ceux d'un homme dont le travail est sédentaire. Tout cela constitue un défi pour la conception des affiches – et il faut choisir soigneusement aussi bien le message pour la santé que les images utilisées pour véhiculer le message.

Comer y moverse. Los carteles de este capítulo muestran muy claramente que los acontecimientos históricos y los factores sociales influyen en los mensajes difundidos por los funcionarios de salud pública. La guerra, las medidas de racionamiento y el declive económico sufrido por Europa en la primera mitad del siglo XX se reflejan en las instrucciones impartidas para no desperdiciar la comida y tomar alimentos producidos en el propio país: "Maíz, el alimento de la nación". Incluso la ciencia que fundamenta esos carteles se ha visto afectada por los conflictos. En el intervalo entre las dos guerras mundiales, los Estados Unidos de América y muchos países europeos participaron en las amplias investigaciones realizadas acerca de los efectos de la dieta y el ejercicio en la salud. Se profundizó en el conocimiento de la calidad y cantidad de los alimentos necesarios para conservar la salud, sobre todo en lo tocante a la función esencial de las vitaminas; de ahí que en varios de los carteles se recomendaran determinados tipos de alimentos, como por ejemplo naranjas o aceite de hígado de bacalao. Las situaciones de guerra llevan a los gobiernos a centrar la atención en la salud y la fuerza de su población. En tiempo de paz, los acontecimientos deportivos permiten a los países exhibir la fuerza y los logros físicos de sus adultos jóvenes, y ese orgullo es algo reconocible en los carteles de China, Ucrania y los Estados Unidos.

La mayoría de los carteles con mensajes sobre lo que se debe comer transmiten esencialmente el mismo consejo, a saber, seguir una dieta diversa y equilibrada, pero ilustrándolo con diferentes alimentos. Los carteles basados en una imagen visual fuerte más que en instrucciones escritas se han de diseñar con sumo cuidado para adaptarlos a la cultura local. Esto es algo que deben tener en cuenta las autoridades de salud pública que se ocupan de las poblaciones de refugiados o inmigrantes, pues a veces los carteles habituales muestran alimentos que los nuevos residentes no pueden tomar o ni siquiera llegan a reconocer. A ello se añade en diferentes países la tensión entre los que tienen demasiado y los que tienen demasiado poco. En el siglo XX, las enfermedades por exceso se han ido revelando tan letales como las asociadas a la privación; puede resultar muy extraño que se recomiende a la población comer y moverse, actividades que damos por supuestas como algo natural.

No obstante, se requieren distintos modos de vida para conservar la salud, según las características de cada persona, de ahí la tendencia a individualizar cada vez más el asesoramiento sobre el régimen alimentario y el ejercicio. Una sesión de ejercicio con efectos tonificantes en una persona puede provocar en otra un infarto o un traumatismo (y nadar en una piscina sucia es peligroso para cualquiera). Las necesidades calóricas de una mujer sometida a un duro trabajo físico no serán las mismas que las de un hombre con una ocupación sedentaria. Estas cuestiones plantean todo un reto para los diseñadores de carteles, pues ello significa que tanto los mensajes sanitarios como las imágenes empleadas para ilustrar esos mensajes se han de elegir con suma atención.

Ешьте и двигайтесь. Плакаты в этом разделе очень четко показывают, что исторические события и социальные факторы изменяют сообщения, распространяемые официальными службами общественного здравоохранения. Война, рационирование и экономический спад в Европе в первую половину 20-ого столетия отразились в инструкциях доедать пищу до конца и употреблять в пищу продукты, произведенные внутри страны; «Зерновые продукты - пища нации». Конфликты повлияли даже на научное обоснование содержания этих плакатов. В период между двумя мировыми войнами Соединенные Штаты Америки и многие европейские страны провели широкие исследования воздействия рациона питания и физических упражнений на здоровье. Сформировалось новое понимание качества и количества пищи, необходимой для поддержания здоровья, особенно понимание важной роли витаминов. Именно поэтому некоторые плакаты рекомендовали конкретные виды продуктов, например апельсины или рыбий жир. Война концентрирует внимание правительств на здоровье и жизнестойкости их населения. В мирное время спортивные мероприятия дают возможность нации продемонстрировать силу и физические достижения ее молодежи, и мы можем видеть гордость за эти достижения в плакатах из Китая, Украины, США.

Большинство плакатов, посвященных питанию, в основном дают один совет: необходимо разнообразное, сбалансированное питание, но они иллюстрируют это с помощью различных продуктов. Плакаты, основанные скорее на сильном визуальном изображении, чем на письменных инструкциях, должны быть глубоко продуманными, чтобы соответствовать местным культурным условиям. Это является важным для органов общественного здравоохранения, занимающихся вопросами беженцев или иммигрантов, так как на обычных плакатах изображаются продукты, которые не известны новым резидентам, или которые они не могут употреблять в пищу. В различных странах существует также напряженность между теми, кто имеет слишком много, и теми, кто имеет слишком мало. В 20-ом столетии стало очевидным, что болезни, связанные с избыточным питанием, так же смертельны, как и болезни, связанные с недоеданием; рекомендация есть и двигаться может показаться странной, так как это действия, которые, как мы считаем, происходят естественно.

Однако различным людям для поддержания здоровья необходимы различные образы жизни и поэтому рекомендации в отношении питания и физической активности становятся все более индивидуализированными. Бодрящие упражнения для одного человека могут стать причиной инфаркта или инвалидности у другого (а плавание в грязном бассейне опасно для каждого человека). Потребности в калориях женщины, выполняющей тяжелую физическую работу, отличаются от потребностей мужчины работа которого малоподвижна. Такие отличия создают проблему для художников плакатов, так как необходимо тщательно отобрать как сообщение о здоровье, *так и* рисунок, иллюстрирующий это сообщение.

吃与动。 从这一章节中的海报中可以清晰看出，历史事件和社会因素可改变公共卫生官员宣传的主题内容。20世纪前半叶，欧洲经历了战争、定量配给和经济衰退。这一点，在要求将饭菜用光和食用国产食物的命令中得到了反映：'玉米：国家之食'。甚至贯穿在这些海报中的科学内容都受到了冲突的影响。两次世界大战之间，美国和许多欧洲国家参与了关于饮食和锻炼对健康影响的大范围研究活动。对保持健康所需食物的质量和数量产生了新的理解，特别是维生素所具有的不可或缺的作用。这也是为何一些海报建议食用特定类型的食物（如柑橘或鱼油）。战争使得政府的注意力集中在人口的健康和体力方面。在和平年代，各国利用运动会来展示青年人的体力和体育成绩。我们可以从中国、乌克兰和美国的海报中看到所反映出的这种骄傲。

这里展示的关于饮食方面的大部分海报从本质上都提出了相同的建议，也就是混合、平衡膳食。但是，利用了不同的食物加以描述。有些海报依靠强有力的视图，而不是书面说明来传递信息，因而应该谨慎设计，使其符合当地的文化习俗。如果新居民认不出或不吃海报上通常描述的食物，这对处理难民或移民事务的公共卫生当局来说就是一个重要教训。在不同国家，富人和穷人之间也存有紧张关系。在20世纪，已经渐渐地证明，饮食过量所导致的疾病与匮乏所导致的疾病具有同等致命性。告诉人们吃了之后再运动，看起来有些怪异，但这是我们认为很自然的事。

要保持健康，不同的人尚需不同的生活方式。因此，关于饮食和锻炼的建议越来越个性化。某人所做的令人精神焕发的锻炼活动，对其他人来讲可能就会引起梗死或损伤（在肮脏的泳池内游泳会给每个人带来危险）。一位从事艰苦体力劳动的妇女所需的卡路里，与一位做办公室工作的男人相比会有所不同。这些问题对海报设计人员带来了挑战，因此，健康主题内容以及用以描述该内容的图画需要进行精心挑选。

إن الملصقات الإعلانية المعروضة في هذا الفرع تبين بوضوح شديد الأحداث التاريخية والعوامل الاجتماعية التي تغير الرسائل المنشورة من قِبَل مسؤولي الصحة العمومية. فحالات الحرب والترشيد والانكماش الاقتصادي التي شهدتها أوروبا في النصف الأول من القرن العشرين كلها مجسدة في الإرشادات الخاصة بإكرام الإناء وتناول الأطعمة المنتجة وطنياً، مثل شعار «الذرة: غذاء الأمة». وحتى العلم الذي استلهمت منه هذه الملصقات الإعلانية فحواها تأثر بالنزاعات التي نشبت. فخلال الفترة الممتدة بين الحربين العالميتين شاركت الولايات المتحدة الأمريكية والعديد من الدول الأوروبية في بحوث مستفيضة في آثار النظام الغذائي وممارسة التمارين الرياضية على الصحة، وخصوصاً الدور الأساسي للفيتامينات في ذلك. وهذا هو السبب الذي جعل العديد من الملصقات الإعلانية توصي بأنماط معينة من الملصقات الإعلانية. وتؤدي الحروب إلى تركيز اهتمام الحكومات على صحة شعوبها وقوتها. وفي أوقات السلم تتيح التظاهرات الرياضية للدول أن تُظهر قوة شبابها وإنجازاتهم البدنية. ويمكننا أن نشاهد هذا الفخر مجسداً على الملصقات الإعلانية القادمة من الصين وأوكرانيا والولايات المتحدة الأمريكية.

ومعظم الملصقات الإعلانية بخصوص الأكل يعطي أساساً النصيحة ذاتها، أي النظام الغذائي المتنوع والمتوازن، ولكنها معروضة مع أغذية مختلفة. أما الملصقات الإعلانية التي تعتمد على الصورة القوية بدلاً من الإرشادات المكتوبة فيتعين تصميمها بدقة كي تناسب الثقافات المحلية. وهذا درس هام لسلطات الصحة العمومية التي تُعنى باللاجئين أو المهاجرين، عندما يُظهر الملصق الإعلاني أغذية لا يمكن أن يتعرف عليها أو يأكلها المقيمون الجدد. وهناك أيضاً شد وجذب في القرن العشرين بين أهل الثراء الفاحش وبين من أدركتهم الفاقة. وفي القرن العشرين ثبت تدريجياً أن أمراض التخمة قاتلة شأنها شأن أمراض الحرمان، وقد يبدو من الغريب للغاية أن يُنصح الناس بالأكل والحركة وممارسة الأنشطة وهي أمور نتوقع منهم أن يقوموا بها بشكل طبيعي.

ومع هذا فإن الأناس المختلفين يحتاجون إلى أنماط حياة مختلفة للحفاظ على صحتهم، ومن ثم فإن النصيحة الخاصة بالنظام الغذائي والتمارين الرياضية تُصبح فردية أكثر فأكثر. فالتمارين الرياضية التي تُدخل البهجة على نفس شخص ما قد تصيب شخصاً آخر باحتشاء عضلة القلب أو تلحق به إصابة ما (والسباحة في ترعة قذرة تُشكل خطراً على كل فرد). والسعرات الحرارية التي تحتاج إليها المرأة التي تؤدي عملاً بدنياً شاقاً ليست هي السعرات الحرارية ذاتها التي يحتاج إليها الرجل الذي يؤدي وظيفة مكتبية. وتطرح هذه المسائل تحديات خاصة أمام مصممي الملصقات الإعلانية، لذا فإن الرسالة الخاصة بالصحة والصور المستخدمة في بيانها لابد من اختيارها بعناية.

天天锻炼身体好

TIANTIAN DUANLIAN SHENTI HAO

■ Daily exercise keeps you fit and healthy. ■ De l'exercice tous les jours, pour rester en forme et en bonne santé. ■ El ejercicio físico diario nos mantiene sanos y en forma. ■ Каждый день физзарядка – вы здоровы и в порядке.

■ التمارين الرياضية اليومية تحافظ على لياقتك وصحتك.

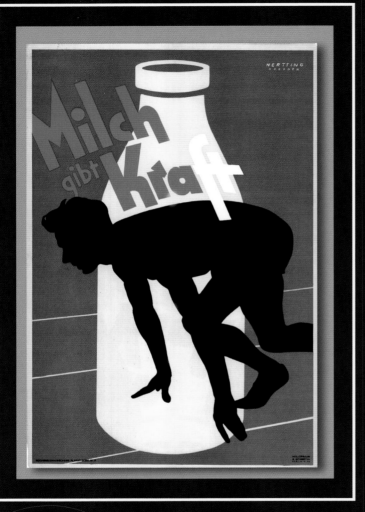

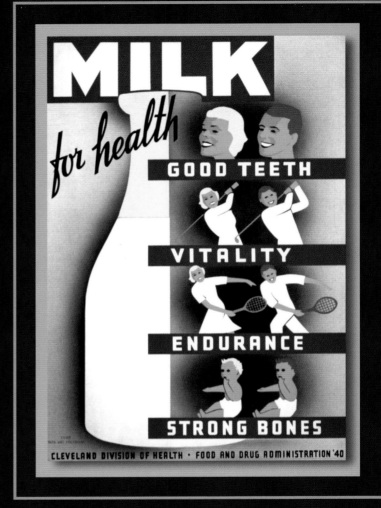

■ Milk makes you strong. ■ Le lait donne des forces. ■ La leche da energía. ■ Молоко дает силу. ■ 牛奶使人强壮。

■ شرب اللبن يمنحك القوة.

■ Du lait pour la santé – bonnes dents, vitalité, endurance, solidité des os. ■ Leche – para la salud (salud bucodental, vitalidad, resistencia, salud ósea). ■ Молоко - для здоровья, хороших зубов, энергичности, выносливости, крепких костей. ■ 牛奶 – 益于保健康、牙齿好、活力强、耐力大、骨质硬。

■ عليكم بشرب اللبن لتنعموا بصحة جيدة وأسنان سليمة والحفاظ على حيويتكم وقدرتكم على التحمل وقوة عظامكم

■ Šipka has some advice for Šibal: If you want to be fit eat fewer cakes and sweets! The sweets may be tempting but fruit is better still! Fruit is good for your health. ■ Sipka a un bon conseil pour Sibal : si tu veux être en forme, mange moins de gâteaux et de friandises. Les bonbons, c'est bon ! Mais les fruits, c'est encore meilleur ! Les fruits c'est bon pour ta santé. ■ Šipka tiene algunos consejos para Šibal: Si quieres estar en forma, ¡come menos golosinas! Los dulces son tentadores, pero la fruta es mejor. ¡La fruta es buena para tu salud! ■ Чтобы быть в хорошей форме, ешьте меньше мучного и сладкого! Если хочется сладостей, ешьте фрукты - они полезны для вашего здоровья.
■ Šipka向Šibal提出建议：身体要健康，就要少食蛋糕和糖果！糖果会很诱人，但水果更佳！水果有益健康。

■ سيبكا لديها نصيحة تقولها لسيبال: إذا كنت تريد أن تتمتع بصحة جيدة قلل من تناول الكعك والحلويات! فالحلويات قد تكون شهية ولكن الفاكهة هي الأفضل! الفاكهة جيدة لصحتك.

149

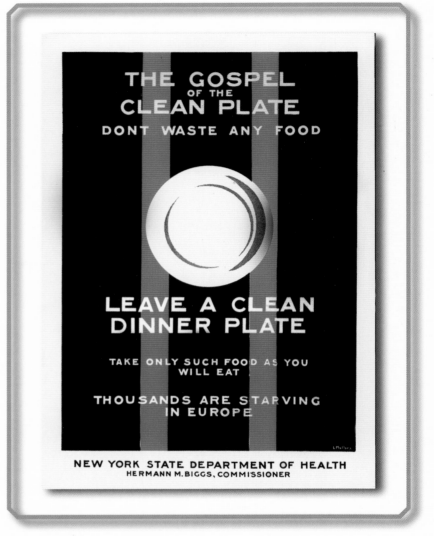

■ Pour aider les femmes de France, ne gaspillez pas le blé. ■ ¿Quiere usted ayudar a las mujeres de Francia? Cada grano de trigo cuenta. ■ Вы поможете женщинам Франции? Спасите пшеницу. ■ 你会帮助法国妇女吗？请节约小麦。

■ هل ستساعدون نساء فرنسا؟ اقتصدوا في القمح.

■ Le principe de l'assiette propre : on ne gaspille pas la nourriture. ■ El precepto del plato limpio: no desperdicie comida. ■ Тарелка должна остаться чистой - это бесспорная истина. Не растрачивайте пищу. ■ 把饭菜用光是行动准则，请不要浪费食物。

■ من تعاليم إكرام الإناء، لا تهدر أي طعام.

■ Ne gaspillez pas la nourriture alors que d'autres ont faim.
■ ¡No desperdicie comida mientras que otros se mueren de hambre! ■ Не растрачивайте пищу, когда другие голодают! ■ 有人还在挨饿，请不要浪费食物！

■ لا تهدروا الطعام وهناك من يتضورون جوعاً!

■ Monsieur, votre femme économise, alors ne gaspillez pas. Finissez ce que vous avez dans votre assiette, c'est la moindre des choses. ■ Señor, no caiga en el despilfarro mientras su esposa trata de ahorrar. Adopte la norma del plato limpio: aporte su granito de arena. ■ Уважаемый, ваша жена экономит, а вы транжирите. Возьмите за правило - все доедать до пустой тарелки. ■ 先生，你的太太爱节约，请你不要浪费。把饭菜用光是采用的信条，你要出一份力。

■ سيدي - لا تهدر الطعام بينما تقتصد فيه زوجتك -
أكرم الإناء - قم بدورك.

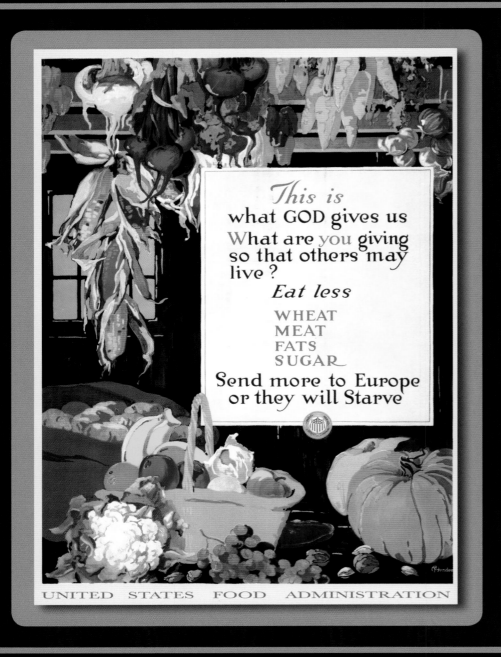

This is
what GOD gives us
What are you giving
so that others may
live?

Eat less

WHEAT
MEAT
FATS
SUGAR

Send more to Europe
or they will Starve

UNITED STATES FOOD ADMINISTRATION

TAKE A PRIDE IN BEING
FIGHTING
FIT

YOU OWE IT TO YOURSELF · YOUR COMRADES · YOUR EFFICIENCY

■ Sois fier de rester en forme pour combattre. ■ Es un orgullo mantenerse en forma para combatir. ■ Будь в форме и гордись этим. ■ 为做到身体强健而感到骄傲。

كن فخوراً بلياقتك البدنية وقدرتك على القتال.

■ C'est ce que Dieu nous donne – et toi que donnes-tu pour que les autres puissent vivre ? Mange moins de blé, de viande, de graisses et de sucre pour en envoyer davantage en Europe sinon ils mourront de faim. ■ Estos alimentos nos los da Dios - ¿Y usted qué da para que otros puedan vivir? Restrinja su consumo de trigo, carne, grasa y azúcar y envíe más alimentos a Europa; sin nuestra ayuda, muchos morirán de hambre. ■ Все это дал нам Бог. А что вы даете, чтобы другие могли жить? Ешьте меньше зерновых, мяса, жира, сахара - посылайте больше в Европу, иначе они умрут от голода . ■ 这些东西由上帝赐给——为了他人的生存，你能提供什么？少食用一点小麦、肉类、脂肪、食糖——多向欧洲送出一些。不然，他们的人会忍饥挨饿。

■ هذه عطية الرب ـ فما الذي تمنحونه كي يتمكن غيركم من الحياة؟ اقتصدوا في أكل القمح واللحم والدهون والسكريات وأرسلوا المزيد إلى أهل أوروبا وإلاّ فإنهم سيموتون جوعاً.

■ Ne gaspille rien, ne manque de rien – prépare-toi pour l'hiver.
■ No despilfarres y no pasarás apuros – preparémonos para el invierno.
■ Не транжирь, не нуждайся - готовься к зиме. ■ 不浪费，不缺少——为过冬做准备。

■ لا تهدري أي طعام حتى لا تصبحي معوزة - واستعدي لفصل الشتاء.

■ Mangeons moins et soyons reconnaissants d'avoir assez pour partager avec ceux qui luttent pour leur liberté. ■ Comamos menos y estemos agradecidos por tener alimentos suficientes para poder compartirlos con quienes luchan por la libertad. ■ Ешьте меньше и давайте будем благодарны за то, что у нас есть чем поделиться с теми, кто борется за свободу. ■ 少吃一点。与为自由而战的人们充分分享，会使我们欣慰不已。

■ لنأكل أقل ولنكن من الشاكرين لأن ما لدينا يكفي لكي نتقاسمه مع من يناضلون في سبيل الحرية.

■ Mamans, n'oubliez pas l'huile de foie de morue, le jus d'orange et le lait. ■ Madres, no os olvidéis del aceite de hígado de bacalao, el jugo de naranja y la leche. ■ Матери, не забывайте про рыбий жир, апельсиновый сок и молоко. ■ 母亲们：请不要忘记鱼肝油、橙汁和奶。

■ أيتها الأمهات - لا تنسين زيت كبد الحوت وعصير البرتقال واللبن.

■ Playing is also learning. ■ Jugar también es aprender. ■ Играть - это также учиться. ■ 玩耍也是学习。

■ العبوا فاللعب يعلمكم أيضاً.

■ Le maïs – la nourriture de la nation. En servir à chaque repas – appétissant, nourrissant, économique. ■ Maíz: el alimento de la nación. Sírvalo en todas las comidas: es sabroso, nutritivo y barato. ■ Зерновые продукты - пища нации. Используйте их в каждую еду – вкусно, питательно, экономно. ■ 玉米——国家之食。每餐必用——用以开胃、补充营养或节俭费用。

■ الذرة ـ غذاء الأمة تناولوها بشكل أو بآخر في كل وجبة ـ إنها فاتحة للشهية ومغذية واقتصادية.

■ Eat green leafy vegetables every day. They are full of vitamin A which is good for your health. ■ Mange tous les jour des légumes verts pleins de vitamine A pour ta santé. ■ Cada día hay que tomar hortalizas de hoja verde, ricas en la saludable vitamina A. ■ Каждый день ешьте зеленолистные овощи. В них содержится много витамина А, который необходим для крепкого здоровья. ■ 天天食用绿色蔬菜。蔬菜富含维生素A，能够保全你的健康。

■ عليكم بتناول الخضروات ذات الأوراق يومياً. إنها غنية بالفيتامين «ألف» الذي يجعلكم موفوري الصحة.

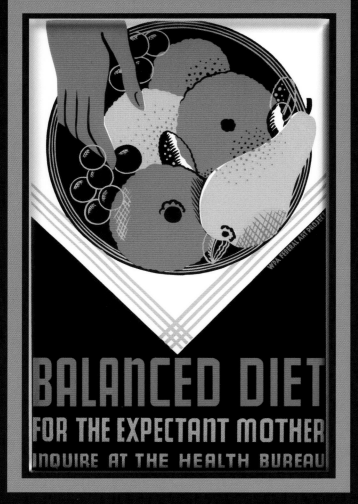

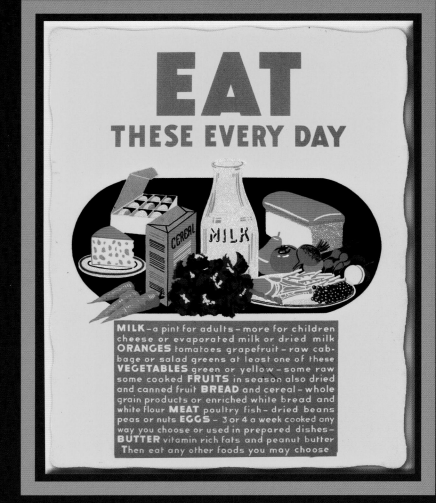

■ Un régime équilibré pour la femme enceinte. Se renseigner auprès du Service de santé. ■ Dieta equilibrada para las futuras mamás. Infórmese en la Oficina de Salud. ■ Сбалансированное питание для будущих матерей. Обращайтесь в отделы здоровья. ■ 孕妇要做到平衡膳食，请向卫生局咨询。

■ الغذاء المتوازن للحوامل عليكن بالاستفسار عنه في مكتب الصحة.

■ Mangez ces produits tous les jours. ■ Coma estos alimentos a diario. ■ Ешьте эти продукты каждый день. ■ 每天都要食用这些食物。

■ تناولوا هذه المواد الغذائية يومياً.

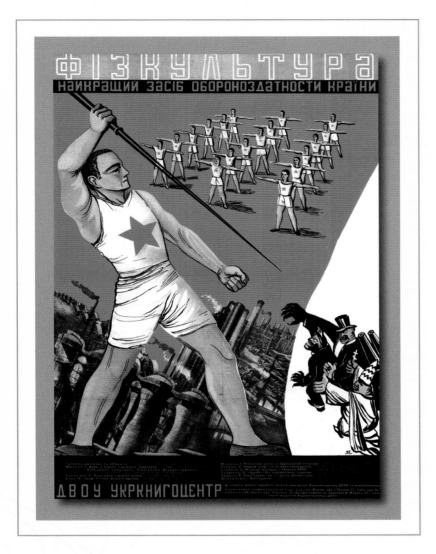

■ Gymnastics. ■ Gymnastique.
■ Gimnasia. ■ 体操.
■ التمارين الرياضية.

■ Nager pour la santé dans des piscines propres et sûres.
■ Nademos por la salud en piscinas seguras e higiénicas.
■ Плавайте на здоровье в безопасных и чистых бассейнах.
■ 游泳健体，要去安全洁净的泳池。
■ لأجل صحتكم اسبحوا في مسابح مأمونة ونقية.

Acknowledgements

Authors

Foreword: *William H Helfand*, New York, NY, United States of America; **Vaccinate:** *Melissa Leach*, Institute of Development Studies, Sussex University, Brighton, England; **Prevent:** *Sanjoy Bhattacharya*, Wellcome Trust Centre for the History of Medicine, University College London, 183 Euston Road, London, England; **Keep clean:** *Valerie Curtis,* London School of Hygiene and Tropical Medicine, Keppel St, London, England; **Protect yourself:** *Claudia Stein*, Department of History, Warwick University, Coventry, England and *Roger Cooter*, Wellcome Trust Centre for the History of Medicine, University College London, 183 Euston Road, London, England; **Don't:** *Anthony D So*, Terry Sanford Institute of Public Policy, Duke University, Durham, NC, USA; **Be Safe:** *Huub Sanders,* International Institute of Social History, Amsterdam, the Netherlands; **Breastfeed:** *Miriam Labbok*, Centre for Infant and Young Child Feeding and Care, University of North Carolina at Chapel Hill, NC, USA; **Eat and move:** *Vanessa Heggie,* Department of History and Philosophy of Science, University of Cambridge, Cambridge, England.

Production

Concept: Laragh Gollogly; **Curatorial assistance**: William Schupbach, Stefan Landsberger, Thomas Hill; **Editing:** Ian Neil, Amanda Milligan; **Editorial support:** Kaylene Selleck, Carla Abou Mrad; **Graphic design:** Sophie Guetaneh Aguettant, Tashira Muqtada; **Quality control:** Christian Stenersen; **Research and permissions:** Yasmin Mohamed, Mary White.

While all efforts have been made to trace the ownership of the images presented in this book and to seek permission for reproduction, it has not been possible to source some of the materials. WHO would welcome any information that enables the Organization to acknowledge these as yet orphan works.

WHO acknowledges the institutions and copyright owners listed below for supplying and giving permission to reproduce the following images indicated by page number and placement (R=right, L=left, C=centre, T=top, B=Bottom):

Centres for Disease Control, Atlanta, GA, USA: 5R, 8 (both Mary Hilpertshauser), 10-12 (Stafford Smith), 13, 37L, 51, 63R, 95R, 95L, 125R, 126L.

National Library of Medicine, Institute of the History of Medicine, Bethesda, MD, USA: 5L, 6R, 7L (Réné Gauch), 9L, 17R, 27L (Lucien Lévy-Dhurmer), 27R (Abel Faivre), 31, 32, 33R, 36L, 37R, 38, 41 (Ernest Hamlin Baker), 56L, 70, 71, 72R, 73L, 76, 77, 84R, 83L, 91R, 99R (G Nicolitch), 98R, 98L, 99L, 100R (V Fekliaev and Plaket Izdatel'stvo), 100R (Alko-Kutt), 102L (Marvel Comics Group/Pew Charitable Trusts), 103R, 106L, 106R, 107L, 107C, 107R.

International Institute of Social History, Amsterdam, Netherlands: 6L, 7R, 14L, 28L, 29, 30L, 48, 49, 50R, 61L, 92L, 92R, 114L, 114R, 116R, 116L, 117L (A Th Schwarz), 117R, 118R, 118L, 119R, 120R (Mendoza), 124L, 128L, 135R, 147L, 149, 150L, 157R.

Wellcome Library, London, England: 36R, 39, 40, 56R, 58, 59, 62R, 69R, 72R, 82L, 101R, 101L, 105 (S Smirnov),115R, 124L, 124R, 126R, 127L, 127R (L Cusden), 128R, 153R, 154R.

Library of Congress, Washington DC, USA: 30R, 35R, 60 (John Buczak), 61R, 62L, 64 (Erik Hans Krause), 69, 113L (Allan Nase), 115L, 118L, 124L, 126L (Earl Schuler), 148R, 150R (Crawford Young), 151L (Edward Penfield), 151R, 152L, 152R (A Hendee), 153 (Land), 154L (Howell Lith), 155L (Lloyd Harrison), 156R, 156L, 157L.

Ministries of Health: 16L (Australia); 14R, 15R (Bolivia); 47-49 (China); 136 (Cook Islands); 94L (Costa Rica); 121 (France); 33L (Ghana); 19R (Honduras); 17L (Indonesia); 75R, 103L (Kenya); 9R (Mexico); 15L, 93L (Morocco); 34R (Mozambique); 20, 61L, 96R, 135L, 136 (New Zealand); 140R (Nigeria); 91L, 138 (Pakistan); 74L (Papua New Guinea); 155R (Philippines); 36, (Russian Federation); 103, 105 (Spain); 137 (Sri Lanka); 97L, 139R (the Syrian Arab Republic); 76, 84, 85 (United Kingdom); 94R, 120L, 128 (United States of America); 139L (Yemen); 34L (Zambia); 104L (Zimbabwe).

United Nations Children's Fund (UNICEF), New York, NY, USA: 16R, 19L, 21L, 28R, 141.

The Royal Society for the Prevention of Accidents. Edgbaston Park, 353 Bristol Road, Birmingham, B5 7ST, UK: 124R, 125R, 126R, 127L, 127R, 129R.

Jane Rabagliati: 115L (Lewitt-Him).

World Health Organization: 35L, 91R, 96L.

Crown Copyright and Public Sector Information: 56R, 58, 71.

Public domain: 39R, 40, 59L, 62R, 98L, 98R, 102R.

The American Lung Association, New York, NY, USA: 37R, 38R, 41L, 56L, 102C.

Brogan and Partners, Birmingham, MI, USA: 79L.

AIDS Resource Center of Wisconsin, WI, USA: 79R.

AIDS Action Committee of Massachusetts, Inc., MA, USA: 84-85.

Texas Department of Health, TX, USA: 83L.

Italian League for the Fight Against Cancer, Rome, Italy: 101R.

National Inhalant Prevention Coalition, Chattanooga, TN, USA: 106, 107 (all Texas Prevention Partnership).

Save the Children, Kathmandu, Nepal: 18R.

PolioPlus, Rotary International, Nigeria: 21R.

Oregon Department of Human Services, HIV/STD/TB Program, OR, USA: 75L.